ALIENS
IN THE FOREST

The Cisco Grove UFO Encounter

By
Noe Torres and Ruben Uriarte

As Told By Donald R. Shrum

Illustrated By Neil Riebe

RoswellBooks.com
Edinburg, Texas

© 2011 by Noe Torres and Ruben Uriarte

ISBN-13: 978-1467945554
ISBN-10: 1467945552

First Edition

Illustrated by Neil Riebe

Front cover art by Joe Calkins of CerberusArt.com

Printed in the United States of America

AUTHORS' NOTE:

This is the only fully authorized account ever written about an amazing 1964 UFO encounter near Cisco Grove, California. Our telling of this incredible tale is with the full cooperation and permission of Mr. Donald R. Shrum, the key eyewitness, his wife Judi, and their son Dan.

DEDICATION:

To the late Paul C. Cerny, the brilliant and dedicated UFO researcher who first worked on this case and who compiled most of the documents and data without which this book could not have been written.

CONTENTS

"...these bizarre humanoid [UFO] occupants exhibit the characteristics of artificial beings.... Consider all the descriptions so far: glowing eyes; glowing bodies; identical appearances; no sex organs; no digestive tracts, no functioning mouths, and no anuses; metallic look; metallic feel; masklike faces with no expression; no discernible emotions; physically cold bodies; hobbling, awkward walks, stiff and mechanical ... hums, buzzes, and clicks for audible communication among themselves, like binary computers. What is the logical conclusion? ... [These creatures] are robots." -- Bruce Rux in *Architects of the Underworld*.

"In most UFO abductions, the victims are subdued easily and taken by the aliens. In my dad's case, he resisted with every ounce of his being and prevailed in the end. He was *not* taken." -- Dan Shrum.

FOREWORD
By Mrs. Donald Shrum

On a dark night in the Tahoe National Forest of Northern California in September 1964, my husband Donald Shrum encountered two unidentified flying objects and spent twelve desperate hours struggling for his life against aliens that seemed determined to abduct him. As I write these words, it has now been nearly 50 years since that fateful night when his bow hunting trip turned into a nightmare. That nightmare still reaches out to us from beyond time and space and continues to affect us to this very day. My husband's strange experience forever changed the course of our lives and, rarely does much time go by without our remembering that horrendous night in 1964.

Following this strangest of all experiences, Don and I sought out answers to our many questions about what happened to him. We turned to scientists, UFO investigators, doctors, the military, and others -- but to no avail. Back in 1964, the kind of experience Don underwent was rare in the annals of human history. Few others on planet Earth had ever experienced such a frighteningly close encounter with these alien visitors and lived to tell about it. We had heard of the 1957 abduction of Brazilian farmer Antonio Villas Boas and the 1961 abduction of Barney and Bet-

1

ty Hill in New Hampshire, but, even so, there was precious little information available to us about the strange phenomenon of alien abduction. It was a confusing and frightening time for us and our families.

Immediately after his UFO encounter, my husband suffered severe emotional trauma of the kind that has been observed in other alien abduction cases that have since come to light, such as that of Travis Walton in 1975. For about a year and a half after the incident, my husband suffered horrible dreams, overwhelming anxiety, and dreadful fears that the strange creatures he encountered in the forest would come back for him again. He was haunted by the sounds and sights that he experienced during his encounter, and the slightest "trigger" brought back a flood of anxiety. The effects he suffered would be called post-traumatic stress disorder today, but that diagnosis was not available back in 1964.

During his battle with the aliens, my husband heard "cooing" or "hooting" sounds like those made by an owl. He thought it was the aliens communicating with each other, and therefore, for years afterward, the hooting of an owl would deeply disturb him.

The strange humanoid beings had horrible dark orbs for eyes that stared menacingly at Don. Those dark, terrible eyes were burned into my husband's memory for a long time afterward. On many a night, he would awaken from a restless sleep, drenched in sweat, and screaming with sheer terror, "Those eyes! Those eyes!" Nobody should have to see the person they love undergo such gut-wrenching anxiety as Don did for nearly two years after his encounter.

As the questions mounted and few answers were forthcoming, our despair grew. There seemed to be no one to whom we could turn -- no one who could help us understand the extremely strange circumstances that had befallen us.

Immediately after the incident, we feared that my husband may have been exposed to radiation, because he returned from the scene of his UFO encounter with strange symptoms that included chest pains, a runny nose, and general fatigue. Since we could not afford to pay for a long series of tests to determine

Don's level of radiation exposure, the doctors told us that all we could do is wait for about two weeks to see if any symptoms materialized. If he had been irradiated, we were told, he would lose his hair, develop blisters, vomit frequently, and experience extreme fatigue. Those were the most traumatic two weeks of our lives, because we were a young couple, just starting out, with a young child and meager finances. I spent sleepless nights wondering what I would do if Don succumbed to radiation sickness. Fortunately, symptoms never appeared.

In the meantime, because my husband worked for a company that built missiles for the U.S. military, we felt that we could not let the story of Don's UFO encounter go public. While it may seem odd to some people, we were convinced that if Don had spoken out about his experience, he would have been ridiculed, and it would have likely cost him his job. It was a different era back in the early 1960s, and companies working on defense contracts for the government were not too interested in hearing that their employees claimed to have encountered "flying saucers," thereby bringing a lot of unwanted publicity to the company and its operations.

We had a baby daughter and were barely getting by financially in those days. Despite the fact that we badly wanted to report what Don had experienced in order to try to find out more about it, we absolutely could not afford for my husband to lose his job. It was as simple as that.

So we remained silent about what really happened that night in the Tahoe National Forest near Cisco Grove, California, in 1964. Over time, we did tell parts of the story to several UFO investigators, but only under the condition that they would not reveal our true identities to the media. My husband's experience had been so unique and so profoundly strange that we feared the inevitable firestorm of publicity and derision. The character assassination of my husband would begin, and his job prospects would be ruined. We would have every curiosity seeker in the world hounding our every footstep, as has happened to many other UFO witnesses.

Back in 1964, there were no agencies to which we could turn for assistance. There were no resources or support groups available to us. Yet, we remained intensely curious about what had happened to Don and desperately wanted answers. Regarding the alien encounter, we wanted someone to answer three very simple questions: who, what, and why.

What brought the UFOs to Cisco Grove? Where did they come from? Who were the creatures that my husband saw in the forest? Why were they trying to abduct him? Those questions remain today, nearly 50 years later, and seemingly, we are no closer to the answers. It's like a jigsaw puzzle with key pieces missing so that you can never see the whole picture, and you don't have enough of it to make an educated guess as to what it is.

After all these years and for the first time ever, we are disclosing in this book the entire story of my husband's amazing UFO encounter in hopes that others may learn from it, that others may finally know precisely what happened to us, and that perhaps, even so many years after the fact, somehow we might be able to gain additional insight into exactly what did happen in that dark forest.

We would like to express our gratitude to the late Paul Cerny, to whom we first told our story, for respecting our desire to remain anonymous. We are also indebted to Ruben Uriarte for his dedication, loyalty and understanding.

Don's health is now failing rapidly, and we have feared that the complete and unadulterated story of his encounter might never be published in book form. We are grateful that this remarkable story, the untold true version, is finally, completely revealed in the pages that follow.

Judi Shrum
November 5, 2011

ONE:
DARK FOREST

In the fall of 1964, one of the world's most intriguing and least known UFO cases occurred in the ruggedly scenic foothills of the Sierra Nevada mountain range in the Tahoe National Forest of Northeastern California. Into this remote wilderness stepped three men from the Sacramento area who planned to spend a relaxing weekend hunting deer with their bows and arrows amidst the pine trees, ravines, and boulders of this rough and tumble region. Little did they realize as their hunt began early on Friday, September 4, that fate would intervene to turn their outdoor recreation into a night filled with sheer terror for one of their number, 26-year-old Donald Shrum of Orangevale, a quiet suburb of Sacramento.

Earlier in the day, Shrum and two co-workers had driven about 70 miles along the old Route 40 that linked Sacramento with Reno, Nevada, before pulling off in the area of Cisco Grove in Placer County. Starting in the area of the Loch Leven lakes, the three hunters gathered up their backpacking equipment, their bows and arrows, and their other supplies and headed into the surrounding trees and hills around the lakes.

This historic area of California is part of the region known as the "Gold Country," for it was here in 1848 that the discovery of gold attracted tens of thousands of miners from all over the world, hoping to strike it rich. Placer County was formed in 1851, its name derived from the Spanish word for sand and gravel deposits that contain gold. In a process called "placer mining," the miners would wash away the gravel with water, thus sifting out the heavier gold ore.

1964 Photo of Shrum Holding His One-Year-Old Daughter Donna (Courtesy of Donald Shrum)

The area around the Sierra Nevada range has also yielded other mineral treasures over the years, including uranium. This fact is interesting to UFO researchers, because rich mineral deposits have often been associated with significant UFO sightings throughout the world. During Donald Shrum's 1964 UFO encounter, as will be further revealed in later chapters, the strange beings that arrived in a UFO were observed by Shrum to be busily engaged in a sort of site survey and seemed to be studying the local flora and fauna.

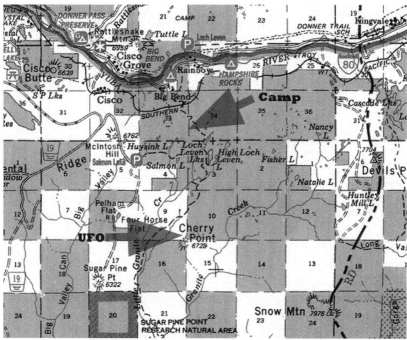

Arrow Shows Area of UFO Encounter
(National Park Service Map)

As in other UFO cases in isolated mountain areas, this Sierra Nevada incident occurred in a zone featuring great diversity in plant life, animal life, and geology. According to scientists, the formation of the Sierra Nevada began more than 100 million years ago, when deposits of granite accumulated deep underground. After an uplift that began about four million years ago, erosion by glaciers exposed the granite and formed the light-colored mountains and cliffs that make up the mountain range. The uplift caused a wide range of elevations and climates in the Sierra.

In terms of wildlife, the area where the UFO encounter happened has long been noted for healthy numbers of deer,

7

mountain lions, bears, raccoons, diverse birds and fish, and much more.

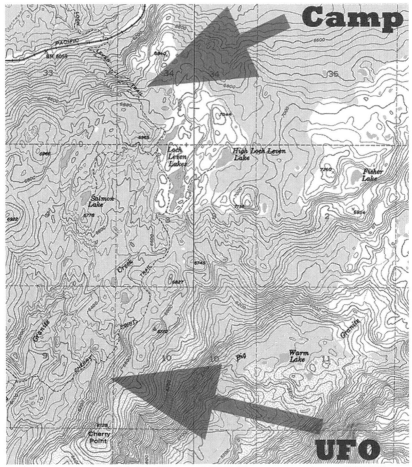

Topographical Map Shows UFO Encounter Area (USGS)

On September 4, 1964, the season for hunting deer with firearms had not yet opened. Donald Shrum and his two companions carried bows and arrows instead as they fanned out across the rocky expanse of trees, brush, and rocks around the Loch Leven lakes. Shrum had been bow hunting for about ten years prior to his UFO encounter. Although he also hunted with firearms, he

8

preferred the bow. "I actually had better luck with the bow than I did with the gun," he said.

The hunters established camp about three miles south of Route 40, near one of the three small lakes, and then went out looking for game. Early in the day, they shot and killed a rattle-snake that lay on the path ahead of them on a ridge. That was to be their only kill of the weekend. Happy to have some time away from work in the great outdoors, the hunters were "confident, cheerful, and happy," according to Shrum.

1964 Photo of the UFO Encounter Area by Don Shrum

"We were getting ready for the evening hunt, and I went down one ridge, one friend of mine went down the canyon bot-tom, and the other went down the other ridge." The men had no walkie-talkies or other means of communication, but kept each other in sight for a while and remained within shouting distance.

Shrum said, "I was on top of this ridge, and the other fellows were down below and they told me to go on around, and they didn't realize it was as far around as it was."

Shrum found that the ridge he was on ended in a steep drop and that he would need to retrace his path and go around it in order to rejoin the others. "When I got to the end of the ridge, it was just a sheer drop off, so I had to backtrack and go down and around the other side of the ridge. By the time I got to the bottom, it was pitch black. And so I stumbled through the brush. I couldn't see anything. It was just dark -- you know, before the moon comes up, it's just really dark in the mountains."

Photo of the UFO Encounter Area, Taken October 1964

October 1964 Photo of Shrum Standing by the Tree He Climbed
(Courtesy of Donald Shrum)

"I got down in this real brushy country. I really got tangled up, and by the time I got out of there it was dark," he said. As the sun had gone down and it was getting dark, Shrum decided he would climb the ridge and seek a safe place to spend the night.

Separated from his hunting party and lost, with night upon him, Shrum did not want to risk wandering around in rugged, unfamiliar terrain in the dark and exposing himself to dangerous animal predators. He had heard reports, in recent days, of bears in the area and did not wish to have an encounter.

"I could see the moon was starting up, and I could see a big granite cliff with a crack that went up the side, and the crack was

11

about a foot wide. So I was able to walk up there, and there was a tree right at the edge when I got up there. I figured there's a lot of bear in the area -- so I figured I would spend the night in the tree.

"The base of the tree to the first limb was about 12 feet, but from the rock it was only about seven feet. I could reach up and hand-walk out to the trunk of the tree and then pull myself up. There were two limbs that came out at an angle, and I sit on one and put my foot on the other one. I was figuring on spending the night up there. I had my bow across two limbs."

According to Shrum, the tree was "close to a mile ... maybe three-quarters of a mile" from their camp, which was "over a mountain."

In setting up a perch in the tree, Shrum followed a common hunters' practice of seeking overnight protection from predators. This practice has kept many a hunter safe from nighttime attacks by bears, coyotes, cougars, and other animals.

Finding a pine tree, about 25 or 30 feet tall, flanked by an outcropping of large rocks, Shrum shimmied up the trunk and tried to make himself as comfortable as possible amidst the rough branches, where he planned to spend the night.

The hunter established his perch in the tree at about sunset, which on September 4 in the Sacramento area occurred at approximately 7 p.m., Pacific Time. About two hours after climbing the tree, Shrum has settled in for what promised to be a long, uncomfortable night when, he saw something very unusual in the sky. The time was around 9 p.m.

He observed a peculiar light in the sky just below the mountaintops to the north of his position. The light was moving from east to west, but it did not follow a straight course, instead seeming to oscillate up and down as it moved west.

Shrum said it "looked just like a flashlight, or a lantern at first, bobbing up and down. But it was below the horizon. I saw it go up over a tree and then down, and I thought maybe it's a helicopter.... I thought my friends had gotten a helicopter from the forest service and figured they were coming out looking for me."

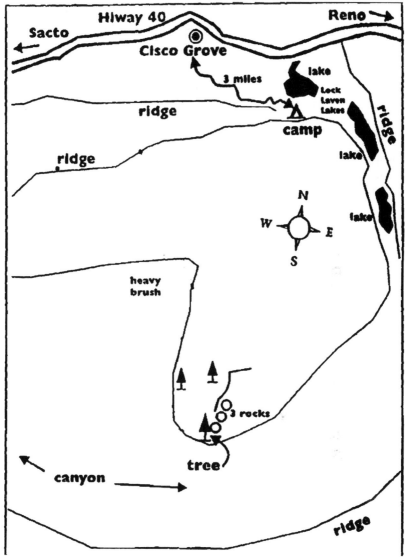

Map Based on Sketch Drawn by Shrum in 1964

Unbeknownst to Shrum, the initial sighting of this strange light signaled the beginning of what would be a desperate 12-hour-long battle for survival against creatures that were clearly not human. The hunter became the hunted, and Shrum's struggle to escape the forest with his life and sanity intact would require all of his wits, his strength, and his courage in the face of an adversary with technology far beyond that of Earth.

What was about to happen would change Don Shrum's life forever. For a long time afterward, what was about to happen caused him recurring fears, paranoia, sleeplessness, debilitating nightmares, and other symptoms seen in individuals diagnosed with post- traumatic stress disorder.

Shrum, who is 73 as of the writing of this book, is still not completely rid of the negative effects of what occurred on this strangest of all nights -- September 4, 1964.

TWO:
HUNTER

Donald Shrum was born in Fayetteville, Arkansas, in 1938, to Edgar Shrum and Imogene Dillard Shrum. After his family moved to the Sacramento area, young Donald attended San Juan High School in Citrus Heights, California. He suffered from scoliosis (double curvature of the spine) and his condition prevented him from obtaining the physical education credits he needed to graduate from high school. Instead, in 1958, he left school to begin working at Pacific Coast Insulation. Drafted to serve in the military in 1958, Shrum was rejected due to his scoliosis.

A year later, in 1959, Shrum got a job as a welder for the Aerojet General Corporation at their Sacramento, California factory, where he worked until 1966. During his time with the company, Aerojet held contracts with the U.S. government to design and build rocket engines for missiles and spacecraft.

Founded in 1942, Aerojet designed and constructed the Titan rocket engines used later for the Gemini space program, the Viking Mars landers, and the Voyager probes to the outer solar system. The company also supplied the U.S. Air Force with its Minuteman missiles, an important part of the nation's missile defense system in the 1960s. In addition, Aerojet built the submarine-launched Polaris missiles for the U.S. Navy.

Most of Aerojet's rocket construction was done at its Sacramento plant, where Shrum worked first as a welder and later as a painter. He recalls painting the hulls of numerous rockets during

15

his years with Aerojet, including the Polaris, MIM-23 Hawk sur-face-to-air missile, and the RIM-7 Sea Sparrow anti-aircraft missile. At the time of the UFO encounter, he was working on Polaris missiles.

Polaris A-1 Missile (USAF Photo)

Shrum also welded the thrust chambers of missiles -- chiefly the Titan missiles. He and a co-worker received an award from Aerojet for their flawless welding work on the booster for Amer-ica's first satellite, Telstar. As part of the welding process, Shrum was frequently exposed to trichloroethylene, or TCE, which was later proven to be a carcinogen and a factor in caus-ing a number of health problems to workers using the substance.

16

*1964 Photo of Donald Shrum Taken at Cisco Grove
(Courtesy of Donald Shrum)*

"The TCE was used to clean parts before welding, and they used basic paint thinners to clean parts before painting," Shrum's son, Dan, said. His father experienced a series of health problems later in life that Dan feels may have been caused by TCE and other "nasty" materials that were in use at the time. Because the dangers involved in using these chemicals were not known at the time, Shrum and his co-workers rarely used safety equipment. Shrum remembers one chemical he used that "burned your throat, even with a full respirator."

Dan Shrum said, "The TCE would make my dad's white shirts yellow and would also yellow the bed sheets. The chemical would just seep out of him through his sweat. My mother also handled his clothing, which was covered in TCE and asbestos powder. It isn't any wonder why she's had medical problems all these years as well."

Aerojet's use of toxic chemicals in the Sacramento area has long been a source of controversy. Their manufacturing, testing and disposal methods led to toxic contamination of both the land and groundwater in the area. Toxic solvents such as trichloroethylene and chloroform and rocket fuel by-products such as N-

Nitrosodimethylamine (NDMA) and perchlorate were discovered in drinking water wells near Aerojet in 1979.

After the extent of the pollution was discovered, two state agencies and the Environmental Protection Agency began working with Aerojet to ensure that the company cleans up pollution caused by its operations at the site.

Some UFO researchers have suggested that these mysterious visitors to our planet might be concerned about humanity's ongoing destruction of our world's natural resources and environment. If this is true, then Sacramento in 1964 would have been an excellent case study for the extraterrestrials.

After his UFO encounter, because he worked with one of the nation's primary defense contractors, Shrum was very hesitant to make his identity known in connection with his UFO experience of September 1964. To further complicate his delicate situation, Shrum's brother, Bill, also worked for Aerojet at that time, as did his friend Vincent A. Alvarez, who went on the deer hunt with Shrum and later testified to having seen the UFO independently of Shrum. The third member of the hunting party, Tim R. Trueblood was also employed by Aerojet.

Fearing retribution from his employer for going public with the UFO story, Shrum asked all the persons he told about the case to refrain from using his real name. "I was afraid that if it got out, they'd think I was a kook and get rid of me," he said. As a result, all of the reports about the case prior to 2005 either omitted Shrum's name or used an alias.

In a January 1965 letter from Shrum's wife, Judi, to UFO researcher Donald Keyhoe, she explained, "We have succeeded so far in keeping the story out of the newspapers because of public ignorance on the subject of UFOs.... My husband works for the missile industry and is afraid of ridicule and possible loss of job."

In addition to fearing for the loss of his job, Shrum obviously also wanted to avoid the public ridicule that was typically heaped upon UFO witnesses starting in 1952 when a CIA-funded study called the Robertson Panel advised the U.S. government to take steps to clamp down on the public's fascination

18

with UFOs. As a result of the Robertson Panel, the U.S. government undertook a public relations campaign to "debunk" UFOs and to reduce public interest in the subject. In addition, the government began closely monitoring civilian UFO groups. Critics say that the Robertson Panel launched a wide scale CIA propaganda effort to push UFO sightings out of the public spotlight and to brand UFO witnesses as "kooks" or persons of a suspicious nature. Some researchers claim that, even as late as the 1970s, the CIA was still using tactics recommended by the Robertson Panel.

J. Allen Hynek, Associate Member of the Robertson Panel in 1952
(U.S. Government Photo)

Presumably based on Robertson Panel recommendations, laws were passed that made it a violation of the Espionage Act for anyone associated with the military to release UFO case files to the general public. Further, Air Force regulation 200-2 stated that all UFO reports were classified and thus could not be released to the public.

Dr. J. Allen Hynek, an associate member of the panel who later became a leading advocate for UFO research, said that the Robertson Panel slammed the lid on UFO research. He said the panel's report "made the subject of UFOs scientifically unrespectable, and for nearly 20 years not enough attention was paid to the subject to acquire the kind of data needed even to decide the nature of the UFO phenomenon." Interestingly, Dr. Hynek later played a small role in investigating the Shrum's UFO case and reportedly ended up in possession of one of the physical artifacts from the Cisco Grove encounter.

Eyewitness Vincent A. Alvarez (right) With His Wife
In Undated Photo (Courtesy of Donald Shrum)

Also experiencing the event with him, to a lesser extent, was his friend and Aerojet colleague Vincent A. Alvarez (now deceased), who was also a missile painter and had worked with Shrum for five years. Alvarez, an avid outdoorsman and bow hunting enthusiast, joined Shrum on the deer hunt that fateful September day. The two men had hunted together for several years, and they were also next-door neighbors later when the Shrums moved to Citrus Heights, California.

The third member of the hunting party was another Aerojet missile painter, Tim Trueblood, who at the time lived in Loomis, California -- located just outside Sacramento. Trueblood, who was more of a friend to Alvarez than to Shrum, worked graveyard shift at Aerojet, whereas Shrum worked day shift and Alvarez worked swing shift.

On September 4, 1964, after Shrum wandered away from his two companions, Trueblood was the only hunter that found his way back to camp on his own. As darkness set in and the other two men had not yet returned to camp, Trueblood decided to leave camp and go looking for them, using his handheld flashlight.

1964 Photo of Tim Trueblood

As Trueblood stumbled out into the darkness shining the flashlight around, Alvarez was attempting to work his way back to camp, when he suddenly noticed a bright light streaking down out of the sky from the upper atmosphere. At first, he thought it might be a slow-moving meteor, but later, after hearing Shrum's story, Alvarez became convinced that he had seen the same UFO that Shrum encountered.

As Alvarez watched the strange object approaching Earth, he suddenly noticed beams of light from Trueblood's flashlight. Moving in the direction of the beams, he soon located Trueblood, and the two men moved back to the camp, where they spent the night. At that point, although they had no idea as to Shrum's whereabouts, they figured that, being an experienced hunter, Shrum would find a safe place to hole up for the night.

After they found Shrum the next day and learned of his ordeal, Alvarez told the others that he too had seen the UFO coming down out of the sky. Later, Alvarez gave a written affidavit stating that he had witnessed the initial appearance of the same UFO that Shrum saw. In the affidavit, Alvarez wrote, "I have worked with Don for five or six years, and knowing him for that length of time, I have no reason to doubt or question his integrity."

Trueblood never made any public statements about the UFO case, and it is assumed that he did not observe anything out of the ordinary on the night in question. Shrum, Alvarez, and Trueblood were all laid off by Aerojet two years after the UFO encounter. Although Shrum kept in close touch with Alvarez for years afterward, he essentially lost track of Trueblood.

Since the three hunters had split up and were at three different locations during the initial sighting, it is possible that, unlike Alvarez, Trueblood actually saw nothing. Some have suggested that perhaps Trueblood chose not to disclose what he saw in order to avoid repercussions.

As of the writing of this book, Trueblood is believed to be living in Hawaii and has chosen to remain silent about this UFO case.

THREE:
MOTHER SHIP

On the evening of September 4, 1964, about two hours after climbing a pine tree in the Tahoe National Forest near Cisco Grove, California, where he intended to spend the night, Shrum observed a strange light moving slightly below the top of a nearby ridge located north of his position. The object moved to below the tree line. At first, the light appeared to be a flashlight or lantern bobbing up and down in the sky and moving from east to west. It formed a distinct orb and did not blink or radiate any outward beams.

As Shrum continued watching, he thought that perhaps the light was a helicopter dispatched from a nearby U.S. Forest Service station. Maybe his two friends had reported him missing and had convinced the park rangers to mount a helicopter search of the area. Perhaps the light in the sky was a helicopter searchlight being employed by the rangers in their effort to locate him down on the ground below. Shrum said, "I saw it go up over a tree and then down, and I thought maybe it's a helicopter from the ranger station."

Not wishing to miss the chance of being rescued, he decided to make his presence known to the approaching airship. Excitedly, he climbed down from his perch in the tree, gathered dry brush and, using matches he always carried with him, lit three signal fires atop three large rocks located near the base of the tree. The three small fires were spaced approximately ten feet apart.

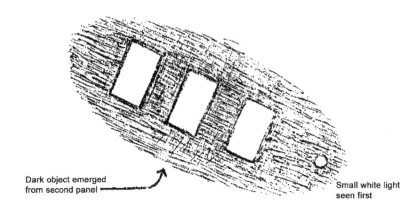

Dark object emerged from second panel

Small white light seen first

Early NICAP Sketch Based on Shrum's Description

Anxious to be noticed, Shrum stood between two of the signal fires and waved his arms eagerly in the direction of the presumed helicopter. "I stood between two of the fires I built on rocks and waved my arms and yelled and screamed ... and finally, that light started coming towards me. So I was really relieved then, because I thought it was a helicopter."

The light, which was at a position northwest of where Shrum stood, suddenly stopped, turned, and moved rapidly toward him. Because night had fallen and the object was very dark, Shrum could not at first distinguish its shape.

The dark object made absolutely no sound as it approached, and, although the craft at first appeared to have only a single light emanating from it, Shrum later noticed three lighted "panels" or "windows" positioned along the side of a hull that he later described as "cigar-shaped." At the forward end of the hull was a small point of light that might be thought of as a "headlight." That the windows were not visible to Shrum at first may have been because they had not opened yet, or perhaps they became visible when the ship turned its side to Shrum.

24

The object, moving northwest to east-southeast, approached silently toward his position at just a bit above Shrum's eye level. Disturbed by the craft's total lack of sound, Shrum became convinced that it was not a helicopter. "That's what scared me," he later said. "I didn't hear any noise at all. The light hovered between two trees and just hung there, and I was pretty sure it was no helicopter." As a person who never thought much about UFOs, Shrum's world was suddenly turned upside down when he suddenly came face to face with what was clearly not an Earth vessel. That this huge ship was not of human manufacture was absolutely clear to him.

It was apparent that the craft approaching Shrum was rigged for silent running. It produced no sound. Its hull seemed to absorb light. Also, the only light that Shrum could see at first was a very small one, which he said seemed like a "fluorescent bulb" except that it could be seen clearly from far away and thus was obviously brighter. The light appeared to only be "about eight inches wide" from Shrum's vantage point.

When he first sighted the object, Shrum could not see the three rectangular panels that became evident later. Because the light at one end of the ship seemed very small and he could not yet make out the overall shape of the object, he arrived at the mistaken conclusion that the ship itself was very small.

"I thought maybe it was just a little dinky thing because I couldn't see anything behind it. I thought of a flying saucer then, but I thought it was just a little tiny one," Shrum said. "I thought it might be something from outer space. But all I could see was about an 8-inch glow -- so I thought it was a little tiny flying saucer."

He did not realize at the time that the small light he was observing was merely the "headlight," a minor component of a much larger ship. The surrounding darkness and the apparent light-absorbing nature of the ship's hull made the size and shape of the object very difficult to judge. Nevertheless, realizing that it was not a helicopter or other conventional aircraft and that it might in fact be a UFO, Shrum decided it would be best to return to the safety of his tree.

"I just threw my bow up in the tree and got up there," Shrum said, "I had camouflage clothing on from head to toe, all the way, hat and everything … and after I got in the tree, I just froze -- just sat as quiet as I could -- thought maybe they couldn't see me, because it was dark in the tree."

The object then made a large, sweeping half-circle maneuver to the east, past Shrum, moving over a nearby canyon on the south side of the ridge. It was now with 50 or 60 yards of his position, hovering over the canyon.

Illustration by Neil Riebe

26

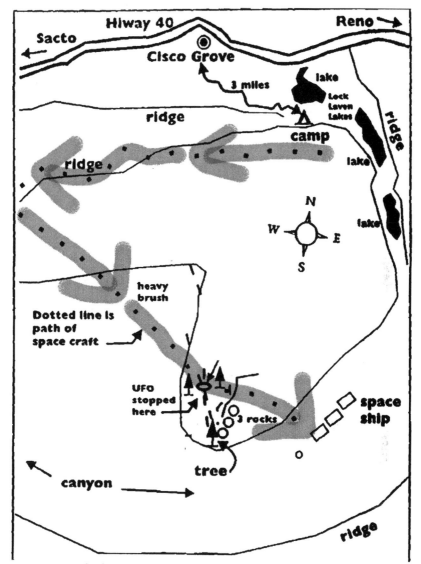

Flight Path of UFO Based on Shrum Sketch

"It made about a half circle around me and got over this canyon, and the moon shone on it. Then I could see, and then it really scared me," Shrum said.

Now, besides the original point of light, he noticed for the first time the three illuminated, rectangular panels arranged in a

27

vertically stepped-down formation. "I could see the shadow of the whole spacecraft. The light was just a light that was on the nose of it. Then I saw three panels of light like windows...."

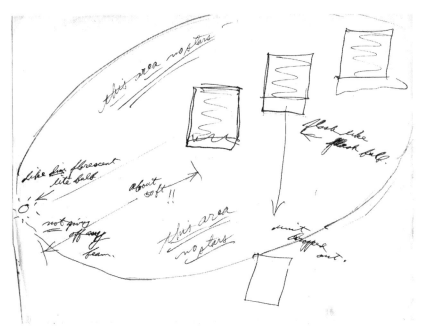

An Early Attempt by Shrum to Sketch the Mother Ship

The illustration above, Shrum's original attempt to sketch the "mother ship," was drawn shortly after the encounter. In it, he makes a guess as to the overall shape of the object based on the fact that he could see no stars behind a roughly oval area within which were contained the three lighted panels In the drawing, he estimates he distance between the single white light that he initially saw coming toward him and the first of the three panels at approximately 50 feet -- adding two exclamation points at the implications for the overall size of the ship. The estimate of 50 feet encompasses only about a third of the total length of the ship, which means that the ship may have been 150 feet in length, equivalent to a 14-story building that had been turned on its side and shot up into the air. Years later, during regressive hypnotherapy, he remembered being startled at the vast size of the object.

Although at first he saw no distinct outline to the ship, he noticed that the stars in the background were being blocked in a rough oval pattern. Later, under hypnosis, Shrum saw the object as more cigar-shaped than it was spherical. After hypnosis, he drew sketches of a more elongated cigar shape for the mother ship.

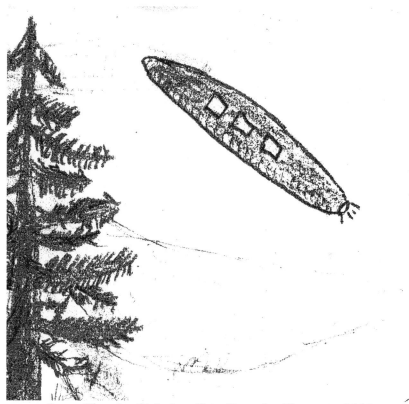

Later Sketch of Mother Ship Done by Shrum in 2000

The lighted panels, which were spaced evenly across the hull of the ship, appeared to be "flat surfaces" from his vantage point. The light emanating from these panels had a strange, shimmering quality, which Shrum described as "like you would take aluminum foil and shake it … wiggle it against the fire … and you would see the glistening, shimmering effect."

He could see nothing attached to either the three shimmering panels or the small light. Everything around these features seemed lost in the darkness of the object itself. Shrum continued observing the strange panels for about four or five minutes, as the UFO remained perfectly stationary, still hovering over the nearby crevasse.

At one point during the encounter, this mother ship zoomed away into the night sky at an extremely high rate of speed before returning shortly thereafter. Shrum said, "I glanced over at the ship that was over the canyon -- kind of almost level with me -- and it was almost out of sight -- it looked just like a star -- it moved that fast, just in that second." Shrum was amazed at the rapid speed at which it moved … and with absolutely no sound.

Shrum's hunting buddy, Vincent Alvarez, although located quite a distance away from Shrum, also saw the UFO, as he later testified. In a written affidavit, Alvarez said, "I also saw the light as I was working my way through the canyon to camp. I got lost too that night."

Shrum also remembers Alvarez stating that he saw the object. "He was telling me the next day that he saw this … he thought it was a shooting star at the time, and it stuck out in his mind that he said, 'Geez, I never saw a shooting star come in that low and last that long.' He was pretty confident that I was telling the truth after that…."

Up to this point in his experience, Shrum had been merely a detached observer of events unfolding before his eyes. Although he had been initially frightened enough to scramble back up his tree, there seemed to now be no immediate serious threat to him.

Unfortunately, something was about to happen that would radically change his situation. His encounter was about to become extremely personal, and instead of being the hunter, he was about to become the hunted. A fight for survival was in the offing, and it would be one that would haunt him for the remainder of his life.

FOUR:
SCOUT SHIP

As Shrum continued to observe the mother ship hovering over a canyon with its three rectangular lighted panels or windows, a very unusual thing happened. "I sat there and watched it -- it must be four or five minutes or so, and then something came out of the second [panel], and all I could see was kind of a flash. Something went straight down the hill," Shrum said.

What he had just observed was the middle panel of the three suddenly flaring or "flashing" almost like someone taking a flash picture. Then, immediately after the flash, a dark object seemed to fall away from the panel, moving quickly down into the canyon below and disappearing into the darkness.

It soon became clear to the witness that this second object was a smaller UFO, which we will refer to as a "scout ship." Shrum called it a "module." It could also be called a "lander." Like the mother ship it came out of, the new vehicle moved in absolute silence, displaying technologies of speed and stealth that were beyond any known to mankind.

Shrum believes that the strange beings he encountered a few minutes later came out of the scout ship, which he thinks later landed perhaps half a mile away from his position. Shrum later explained, "It went pretty fast I saw a big flash of light as it left. I couldn't tell what it was. I just saw a dark object shoot right down, and there was a flash when it came out."

Illustration by Neil Riebe

"I saw something come out of the center [panel] and go straight down the canyon and couldn't see it. It was dark down there. And I didn't bother much about it -- just kept my eyes on the [mother ship]."

A short time later, the scout ship zoomed past Shrum along the north side of the ridge, and he began to understand that it also was a flying vehicle and that it had been disgorged from the larger mother ship. "I saw this little blinking light, and I could see just a ... part of a dome on top and just a little light flashing on it."

Shrum added, "I couldn't tell what shape it was or anything. I just see a dark object shoot right straight down, and there was a flash when it came out of the second [panel], and then I never saw it any more until I saw the light up on the hill. I just figured that was it."

The silver-domed scout ship with its blinking light became stationary up on the side of a nearby hill, a distance of perhaps half a mile from Shrum's position. He thought it had landed, although he could not tell if the ship was actually on the ground.

32

Shrum said, "When it landed up on the ridge, I could only see part of the top, but it had a little light on it and looked like the top of a flying saucer that I'd seen in pictures ... like a dome."

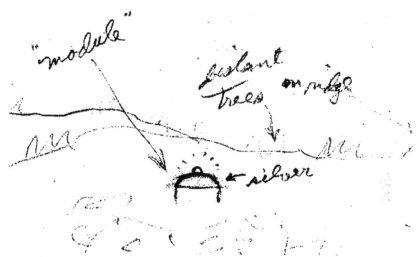

Shrum's Sketch of the Smaller UFO, Which He Called the "Module" (Courtesy of Donald Shrum)

Shortly after the scout ship became stationary, Shrum heard a "crashing through the brush down the mountainside" as if a party of unknown individuals was trudging down the slope toward him. The sound of someone (or something) crashing through the brush toward him continued for about five or ten minutes. Little did Shrum realize that the beginning of his encounter with the "aliens" was now only moments away.

During most of the approximately twelve hours that his encounter lasted, both the scout ship and the mother ship remained fairly close at hand. At one point in the encounter, the scout ship seemed to move higher up the hillside, but generally, it stayed in the same vicinity as if standing by for its imminent departure and return flight. Also during the ensuing battle, the mother ship zoomed far up into the night sky at a high rate of speed, only to return later.

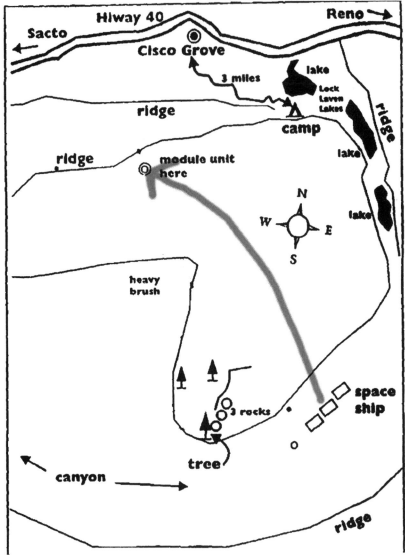

Illustration Shows Path of Scout Ship After Leaving Mother Ship

Estimating from Shrum's sketch of the mother ship and its rectangular panels, each panel might have been about 30 feet long and perhaps 20 feet wide. This allows us to make a rough guess as to the maximum size of the scout ship, which had to fit through one of these portals.

*Artist's Conception of the Domed Scout Ship with Blinking Light
on Top (Courtesy of Donald Shrum)*

This smaller ship, Shrum believes, might have held as many as six humanoid beings and two other entities that he described as "robots." These creatures were about to make their appearance at Shrum's improvised hiding place, the tall pine tree within which he was hiding, hoping to go unnoticed.

It is significant to note that in 1964 the U.S. space program was still very much in its infancy, and the concept of a "mother ship" and a "lander" were not widely known to the American public, as those ideas were not introduced until the first Apollo mission in 1967.

Humankind's first tentative steps into outer space, while commendable, betrayed a very low level of sophistication in

35

1964. The Mercury flights essentially consisted of a tiny manned capsule carrying a single astronaut strapped atop a ballistic missile. The first two Mercury missions were boosted into space by a modified Redstone missile, derived from the German V-2 rocket, which might have won World War II for Germany if its scientists had been given more time and resources to develop it. The German technology fell into U.S. hands after the war.

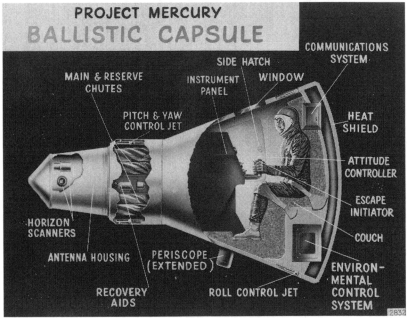

NASA Photo of Mercury Space Capsule

The Mercury manned spaceflights, with their single astronaut inside a tiny capsule, had ended in May 1963 after astronaut Gordon Cooper, who later admitted to having had several UFO sightings during his military career, successfully completed 22 orbits of the Earth and then executed a harrowing manual reentry before splashing down safely in the Pacific Ocean.

Following the first two Mercury missions, NASA began using a modified Atlas intercontinental ballistic missile to boost the remainder of its Mercury spacecraft into Earth orbit.

NASA Photo of Saturn SA-7 Launch on 9-18-1964

In 1964, the U.S. space program was in the midst of a two-year hiatus, during which preparations were being made for the Gemini two-man space flights that, ironically, were boosted into space by Titan rockets designed and built by Aerojet, the company that employed Donald Shrum in 1964. In fact, Shrum did some of the welding on the Titan's thrust chambers.

Also in 1964, testing began in earnest on the Saturn rockets that would eventually take astronauts to the moon. Interestingly, one week after Shrum's UFO encounter, on Friday, September 18, 1964, NASA launched the Saturn SA-7 unmanned test mission from pad 37B at Cape Canaveral, Florida. Among the SA-7's notable achievements was that it carried aboard the very first programmable computer ever used in space flight. A number of other Saturn rocket launches were conducted in 1964.

NASA Photo of Gemini Docking Exercise

These were heady moments for the U.S. manned space effort, but regardless of the rapidly improving liquid-fueled designs of the era, the crude rockets were nothing more than modified intercontinental ballistic missiles. The early U.S. astronauts, in the words of author Tom Wolfe, were expected to sit "on top of an enormous Roman candle, such as a Redstone, Atlas, Titan or Saturn rocket, and wait for someone to light the fuse." The technology used for these early flights must have seemed extremely primitive to Shrum, as he observed the incredible alien ships that surrounded him in the Tahoe National Forest on September 4, 1964.

The first Gemini space mission launched on March 23, 1965, and the first successful docking of two spacecraft took place one year later, during the Gemini 8 mission of March 1966. None of the crude aerospace technology of the U.S. space program in the

1960s came close to the capabilities that Shrum saw displayed by the strange spacecraft on the fateful night of his 12-hour battle with the aliens.

FIVE: HUMANOIDS

As already noted, Donald Shrum observed a smaller ship coming out of one of the rectangular hatches on the mother ship. This smaller craft at first moved downward into the shadows of a nearby canyon but then zoomed past him and assumed a stationary position to the northwest, on the side of a hill. Shrum at first described the object as "dark," and it was likely constructed of the same light-absorbing material of which the mother ship was apparently made. Later, illuminated by the moon and a small light on it, the scout ship seemed to Shrum to be silver in color.

This scout ship appeared to be generally dome-shaped, with a small, white blinking light atop the dome. Given the estimated dimensions of the panel out of which it came, the scout ship was probably no more than 30 feet wide and possibly 20 feet high.

Shortly after the object became stationary to the northwest of his tree, Shrum began hearing what he described as "all this crashing through the brush down the mountainside."

A few minutes later, Shrum saw a short, stocky being, which he later referred to as a "humanoid," approaching his tree from the northwest, emerging from an area of thick vegetation. Standing approximately five feet tall, the creature was dressed in a tight-fitting, light-colored uniform, possibly a whitish silver color. The uniform appeared to be one piece, and it had "bellows" at the elbows and knees of the suit. "They were human in form and … they seemed awfully short, you know, short, stocky," Shrum said.

Illustration by Neil Riebe

The creature's head was covered by either a tight-fitting hood or a helmet. Its face was dark and featureless. The only striking characteristic that Shrum could discern were two large, circular eyes that made it seem as if the creature was wearing welder's goggles. The eyes, like the rest of the face, seemed void of detail.

Moments later, a second humanoid appeared, dressed identically. The illustration that follows shows the straight path taken by two humanoids from the scout ship, through a thick growth of brush, and on to the area around Shrum's tree. It did not seem to bother the creatures that they had to trudge through very dense brush, and later in the evening, the humanoids retreated toward the safety of the brush when they felt threatened by Shrum.

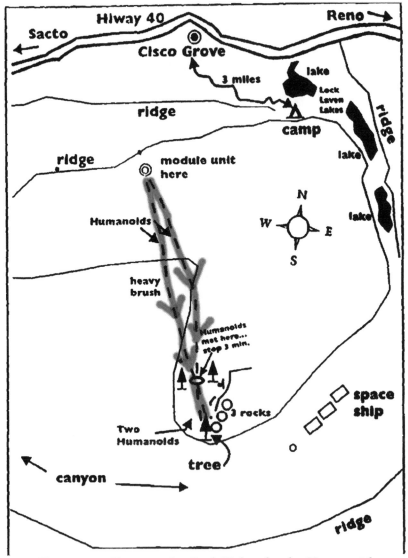

Illustration Showing the Path Taken by the Humanoids

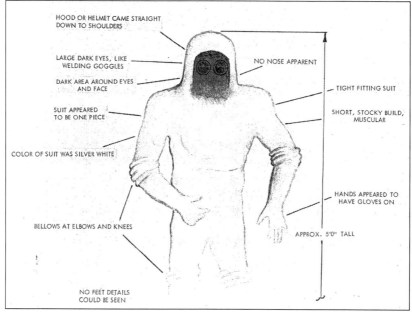

HOOD OR HELMET CAME STRAIGHT
DOWN TO SHOULDERS

LARGE DARK EYES, LIKE
WELDING GOGGLES

NO NOSE APPARENT

DARK AREA AROUND EYES
AND FACE

TIGHT FITTING SUIT

SUIT APPEARED
TO BE ONE PIECE

SHORT, STOCKY BUILD,
MUSCULAR

COLOR OF SUIT WAS SILVER WHITE

HANDS APPEARED TO
HAVE GLOVES ON

BELLOWS AT ELBOWS AND KNEES

APPROX. 5'0" TALL

NO FEET DETAILS
COULD BE SEEN

*Paul Cerny's Sketch of One of the Humanoids,
Based on Shrum's Original Sketch*

Describing the initial appearance of the first humanoid, Shrum later said, "After about five or ten minutes of the crashing through the undergrowth, I saw this first … person, or some kind of a guy all in some kind of light-colored, silver or whitish-looking uniform, with kind of puffs around the sleeves and joints."

The first creature stopped about a hundred feet northwest of Shrum's position and seemed to be studying or gathering samples from a Manzanita bush nearby. Manzanita is a common evergreen shrub found throughout the western U.S. There are 106 different species of Manzanita, 95 of which are found in the mountainous areas of California. Some Manzanita species are among the rarest plants in the world.

Shrum said, "It came within, I guess -- oh, a hundred feet … stopped and [began] messing around with the Manzanita and stuff, and I don't know what it was doing -- looking -- or what it was doing. And then it was joined by another one just like it."

43

The creatures seemed to be intensely "curious" about their surroundings.

Shrum described his initial reaction to the appearance of the UFOs and the humanoids as "pure panic." He was "scared to death" of what he was seeing. His lifelong indifference about UFOs ended immediately, as he saw the two unearthly figures moving around in the brush near his tree.

According to Shrum, he immediately shifted into survival mode, asking himself the question, "What can I do to survive this situation?" His immediate thought was that, dressed in full camouflage gear and partially hidden among the foliage of the pine tree, perhaps he could be quiet and still -- and remain unnoticed by the creatures.

His approach seemed to be working for him, when suddenly, one of the humanoids ceased its exploration of the nearby brush and moved to the base of Shrum's tree. Moments later, the second humanoid joined the first, and they both stared up at him. "They came down right below the tree, at the base of the tree, and were looking up at me. And they had real large eyes -- eyes as big as silver dollars." Shrum was frightened by those dark eyes. He was especially remembered their large size and the fact that they seemed more like round welders' goggles than normal eyes.

For nearly two years after the encounter, Shrum would often awaken late at night from nightmare-plagued sleep, screaming at the top of his lungs, "Those eyes! Those eyes!" According to Mrs. Shrum, the frightening memory of those dark, menacing eyes remained with her husband for a long time after his UFO experience.

The beings were now standing at the base of his tree, only about twelve feet "straight down the tree" from his perch amidst the branches. Both beings had obviously seen him and were looking up at him. "I knew my cover was blown," he said.

"All I could see was a black, flat-looking face with big, dark eyes," Shrum said, "I couldn't tell the color -- they seemed extra large. And their face was just kind of black-looking. I couldn't see if they had a helmet on or not.... All I could see was a black patch of face, and the eyes. I couldn't make out any features of the face."

The creatures also seemed to have a nose that was extremely flat and was located much lower on the face than in a human. This was an unusual feature that Shrum remembered later when he talked with UFO investigators. "It seemed like [the nose] was awful low on their face, low and flat," he said.

As the creatures looked up at the tree, it seemed that they were uncertain what to do, or perhaps they were awaiting further instructions. It was at this time that Shrum noticed that the humanoids seemed to be receiving some kind of audio communications from the mother ship, which still hovered nearby.

Shrum heard strange "cooing" or "hooting" sounds ("like an owl would make") that seemed to come from the humanoids, with a similar sound seemingly emanating from the hovering mother ship. He described the phenomenon as a "signal set-up" between the creatures and their principal ship.

"At the time, I thought that the humanoids turned their heads toward the mother ship every time they heard this noise," Shrum said. "They would look up at the sky [toward the ship]. So I thought at the time that this was their way of communicating."

As the night went on, Shrum noticed that every time the humanoids received a communication from their ship, they would initiate a new course of action. One could make an analogy to the helmet headsets worn by football quarterbacks in order to receive instructions from their coaches on the sidelines. Clearly, the humanoids' actions were being orchestrated by other beings aboard the mother ship.

"Every time this noise would come from the ship … they would do something else," Shrum said. "I just connected it [the sounds with the creatures' actions]. It might have been some owls some place, but I connected it."

For the rest of his life, Shrum associated the sounds of owls with his UFO experience. During later camping excursions, he would often become startled and anxious upon hearing an owl.

The humanoids seemed to have an agenda that involved exploring the immediate area and possibly collecting samples or analyzing the plant life. As Shrum looked on from his perch in the tree, the humanoids thrashed around the surrounding brush, examining rocks and plants, and generally ignoring their human observer. Obtaining a human specimen was not part of their original mission, or so it would seem. Shrum later said, "It seemed like they were scouting for something -- looking around for something. I don't know what."

Original Sketch by Shrum of Humanoid
(Courtesy of Donald Shrum)

Eventually, later in the night, the two humanoids that had originally appeared were joined by perhaps as many as four others, although only the first two approached Shrum's tree. He said, "I could see there must have been I guess five or six of the ones in white ..... I could see them [the others] out going over a rock every once in a while or hear them out in the brush thrashing around."

46

He wasn't completely certain of the exact number of humanoids, although he felt certain there were at least four altogether and perhaps as many as six. As the creatures wandered in and out of the surrounding brush, it was difficult for Shrum to tell whether he was seeing different humanoids or the same ones he had previously seen. "I'd say there were five or six [humanoids] altogether. I might have seen the same one several times, I don't know," Shrum said in a later interview.

Shrum saw another, distinctly different creature arrive on the scene shortly after the appearance of the first two humanoids. "Then I heard this other crashing around me all just over a little bit where they [the humanoids] were, and I saw these big eyes coming just like two flashlights hooked together." It was a vision that would haunt him for a long time afterward.

The creature he called a "robot" was arriving, and his battle against these strange beings was about to begin.

SIX:
ROBOT

The first two humanoids to arrive on the scene moved up to the base of Shrum's tree and stood there, staring up at him. Moments later, Shrum heard another "trashing" sound coming from the nearby brush just north of his position. This sound was coming not from the thick vegetation from which the humanoids had appeared; but rather, from a more easterly different direction, along a nearby ridge.

Turning to look in the direction of the new sound, Shrum saw two huge eyes coming toward him "just like two flashlights hooked together." These glowing, luminous eyes were reddish-orange ("the color of fire"), and they illuminated the face and the jaw of a horrific robot-like creature that rapidly approached Shrum's position. Below the glowing face, from the neck down, he could not see much detail.

The eerie, incandescent eyes had a frightening quality that greatly troubled and unsettled Shrum. The newly arrived creature either was clothed in a metallic-looking suit that made it look like a robot, or perhaps it actually was a robot. Except for its metallic appearing suit and different facial features, the new creature resembled the humanoids that Shrum had seen earlier. Both types of beings were about five feet tall, with the humanoids being perhaps slightly taller. Both types seemed "short and stocky" and had circular, goggle-like eyes.

Illustration by Neil Riebe

The creature Shrum refers to as a "robot" had reddish-orange eyes, no apparent nose, and a large mouth and square jaw mechanism. He called it "a hinged jaw or something," and added that the creature's head "looked metal or dark gray of some kind." Also, its hands resembled human hands wearing the gloves from a suit of armor and appeared hinged at the finger joints.

Where there were a few differences in appearance between the "robot" and the "humanoids," there were also quite a few similarities. It is possible that both kinds of creatures were robotic entities, and it is also possible that they were both biological organisms. As to their relative heights, it was difficult for Shrum to judge, because he was looking down at them from his perch in the tree, about twelve feet off the ground.

While the humanoids moved fluidly, as humans do, the movements of the robot were a lot stiffer and appeared mechanical. Shrum said the way the robot moved and walked was not "flexible" as were the humanoids. The use of the term "robot" was derived from Shrum's general impression of the creature's appearance and movements.

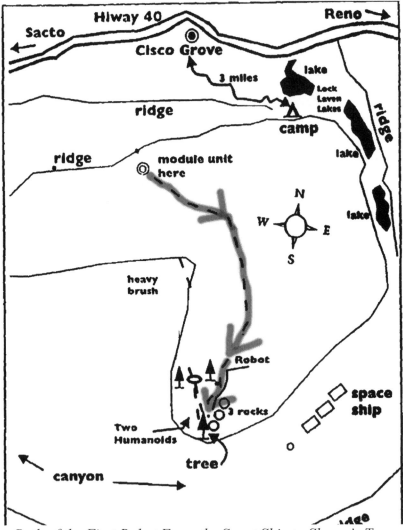

Path of the First Robot From the Scout Ship to Shrum's Tree

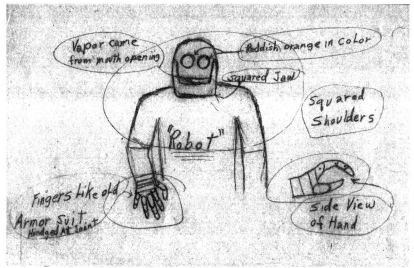

*Original Sketch by Shrum of Robot Creature
(Courtesy of Donald Shrum)*

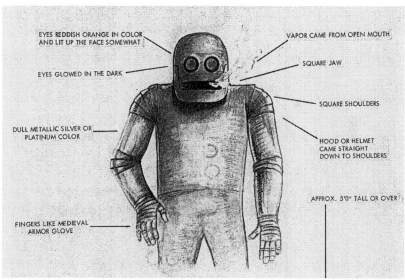

*Paul Cerny's Enhancement of Shrum's Original Sketch of the
Robot*

Interestingly, according to a sketch drawn by Shrum shortly
after the incident, the robot took a different route from the scout

ship to the tree. The robot avoided the dense brush that the two humanoids had thrashed their way through.

The robot, perhaps after communicating with the humanoids, took a smoother path slightly east of the brushy area. It seemed to be "just picking its way down the ridge, between the rocks, and around them."

"It come down -- right down the ridge instead of up the canyon like they [the humanoids] did -- and it stopped right on top of the rocks, just out in front of me," Shrum said.

The robot came right up under the tree "and stood there for awhile." The two humanoids remained close by, also near the base of the tree. According to Shrum, the creatures were "just looking ... staring. They weren't doing anything else."

Moments later, the hunter noticed that the robot was moving toward the remnants of one of the signal fires he had made back when he thought the light in the sky might be a helicopter. By this time, the fire had died down, and only a few embers still glowed there on top of one of the rocks.

As Shrum observed, the robot positioned itself right alongside the rock containing the embers, as shown in the next drawing made by Shrum, and reached out one of its long arms to sweep off and scatter the remains of the signal fire that Shrum had built.

"The fires I had built were just kind of cold then, and [the robot] took its arm and went through them ashes ... and scattered them all over the place," Shrum said.

Shrum made a mental note of the creature's apparent aversion to fire. Its action to sweep the embers off from the top of the rock might indicate a fear of, or uncertainty about, fire. Shrum stored this observation in his memory for possible use later. As it turned out, this would be an important fact that he would later use against the creatures when his battle for survival began in earnest. Deprived of any significant weapons, Shrum had to rely on his cunning to survive what lay ahead.

As the robot swept off the embers, Shrum got a good look at the hand. "It was in joints, but it was like a hand ... fingers and everything." He added that it looked like a "Medieval metal gauntlet." This could indicate that either the creature was wearing a glove or that its hand was metallic (robotic) in composition.

Shrum continued observing the robot. "I could see the face fairly plain because of the eyes lighting up.... I couldn't see much detail from the neck down. It was just a general shape, that's all."

Drawing by Shrum Shows Him in the Tree and the Robot Below, Standing Partly Behind a Large Rock and Sweeping the Embers

Since the robot and the humanoids seemed busy in some kind of mission of exploration, the strange beings appeared at first to be leaving Shrum alone to oversee things from his tree. This would soon change, though, and it would change very quickly. At a later point, apparently after receiving additional instructions from the mother ship, the creatures made Shrum their prime target.

As a footnote to the appearance of this strange robot-like creature, quite a number of other UFO witnesses have reported seeing entities that resembled robots (See Appendix C). Typically, the beings associated with UFOs are described as being organic in appearance, although they seem to not have digestive or reproductive organs and might be genetically "manufactured" or cloned for space travel.

Interestingly, there was a reported "robot" sighting during another UFO encounter less than a year after the Shrum case. The second case occurred on March 2, 1965 near Brooksville, Florida, located about 45 miles north of Tampa, and involved an eyewitness named John F. Reeves.

The 66-year-old Reeves, a retired longshoreman who had moved to Florida in 1961, claimed to have seen a "big flying saucer" that had landed in an open clearing near his home. He crawled through thick brush and approached to within 100 feet of the craft, at which point he observed a strange creature that he called a "robot."

In a letter she wrote in 1965 to UFO researcher Donald Keyhoe, Shrum's wife, Judi, compared her husband's encounter to the Reeves UFO case in Florida. She wrote, "My husband had a very weird experience with an UFO and its inhabitants in September of 1964 while hunting for deer with two other men off highway 40 at Cisco Grove in California.... His experience is similar to the one of the longshoreman Mr. John F. Reeves in Brooksville, Florida. My husband's experience, though, was with two robots and five short, stocky men with light-colored uniforms."

SEVEN: WHITE VAPOR

Still watching from his perch in a pine tree, about twelve feet off the ground, Donald Shrum saw the strange robot sweep away the embers of his signal fire from the top of one of the nearby rocks. Then, the robot moved stiffly back toward the base of Shrum's tree and positioned itself directly below his hiding place. It now stood about seven feet from where Shrum was hiding. What happened next was shocking and unexpected to the experienced outdoorsman.

Apparently after being directed to do so by its handlers in the nearby mother ship, the robot moved one of its hands up to the square-jawed, hinged mouth on its metallic head. As the two humanoids stood nearby watching, something the robot did with its hand suddenly caused a cloud of white vapor to spray out of its mouth, quickly forming a cloud that moved up toward the startled Shrum.

"It put one hand up to its mouth … and some kind of white vapor came out," Shrum said. "He was upwind from me, so it just came up through the tree and acted like nitrogen would, just (like) gas …. I never did smell anything. There was no smell of any kind, but I just kind of gasped for breath and then I blacked out and fell across my bow."

The vapor, which was odorless, had an immediate effect on Shrum, causing him to gasp for breath and black out within seconds. Based on Shrum's description of the effects of the gas, it was likely an asphyxiant. Asphyxiant gasses, which are relatively inert and odorless, reduce or displace the normal levels of oxygen in breathable air, thereby increasing the amount of carbon dioxide in the blood. Typical asphyxiants include nitrogen, argon, and helium. While asphyxiants are normally non-toxic or minimally toxic, because they reduce the oxygen levels in the air, they can lead to suffocation.

Illustration by Neil Riebe

While our planet's atmosphere is made up of 79 percent asphyxiant gasses, chief of which is nitrogen, adverse effects on humans are prevented by the 21 percent oxygen content. However, when asphyxiant levels are increased in the air being breathed by a human, that person suffers from oxygen deprivation (or "hypoxia"), as seems to be the case with Donald Shrum during his struggles with the aliens.

October 1964 Photo of the Tree Shrum Climbed
(Courtesy of Donald Shrum)

The fact that an asphyxiant was used in an attempt to subdue Shrum may indicate that the aliens wanted a pristine, unharmed human specimen for whatever purposes they had in mind. If they had used any sort of toxic gas, Shrum's biological functions would have been seriously compromised, possibly to the point of death. Clearly, they wanted him alive for reasons that remain unclear to this day. However, Shrum is convinced that, once captured, he would have been subjected to the same suffering that other abduction victims have undergone. "Definitely they were trying to hurt me," Shrum said many years later, reflecting on his experience in 1964.

As it turned out, the launching of the gas was the opening volley of a battle that would continue all through the night between Shrum and the alien creatures. Before the robot disgorged the white vapor for the first time, causing Shrum to black out, the hunter was planning to just sit tight up in his tree and take no action against the strangers. "I was going to be peaceful and quiet before that," he said. Now, he realized he was in a struggle for his life and future well-being.

His agenda was to make it out of the forest alive and of sound mind. The creatures' agenda, he could only guess at. Although initially they had essentially ignored the fact that he was up in the tree observing all their activities, obviously there had now been a change of strategy on their part.

Were they trying to abduct him? Did they consider him just another sample of the native life on the planet? Were they interested in experimenting on him in the same manner that he had observed them tinkering with some of the nearby plants and rocks?

Perhaps they initially ignored Shrum because he was a random factor that they had not expected to encounter in such a remote wilderness. Maybe the programming of their mission objectives did not include any contingencies for dealing with the sudden, unexpected introduction of a random variable. In this view, Shrum acted as the proverbial "fly in the ointment" that nobody had counted on.

UFO researcher Donald B. Hanlon, writing in the British publication *Flying Saucer Review* in 1966, suggested that the aliens may have been trying to ensure that Shrum did not interfere with whatever their original mission was. "The all-night harassment of the young Californian can be interpreted as an effort to confine his activity and observation to a limited area," Hanlon wrote. "The witness claimed to have seen … other 'men in white' moving about the area at various times during the night, who were apparently unconcerned with the scene being enacted at the foot of his tree. It may be assumed that some type of operation was being undertaken in this region and that the witness' presence would have hindered these activities."

However, Shrum believes that the aliens, at some point, changed their original strategy of ignoring him and decided it would be worth their while to collect a human specimen. Looking at the overall sequence of events, it appears that eventually someone -- most likely someone aboard the mother ship -- decided to capture Shrum, since the opportunity had presented itself. Once the decision was made, the robot immediately executed the new playbook, uncorking the strange white vapor that drifted up into the pine tree and rendered Shrum unconscious. "I figured they were out to get me," he said later.

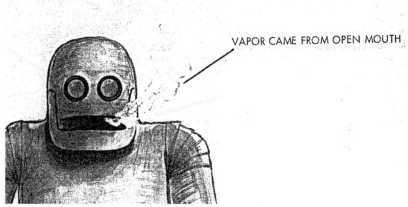

VAPOR CAME FROM OPEN MOUTH

Sketch of Robot by Paul Cerny

Hanlon wrote, "Possibly the oddest feature of this entire story is the method in which the 'robot' expelled the 'knock-out' vapor." Hanlon cited two other UFO cases that involved a similar, mysterious vapor – a 1947 case in Villa Santina, Italy, and a 1952 case in West Palm Beach, Florida involving a scoutmaster named Sonny Desvergers.

In the Italian case, an artist was painting outdoors near Villa Santina when he witnessed the landing of a 30-foot-diameter flying disc in a nearby clearing. Immediately after the ship arrived, he saw two small humanoids, about three feet tall, wearing dark blue coveralls and a bright red collar and belt. The artist, still holding his paintbrushes in his hand, made a gesture of greeting that apparently seemed threatening to the visitors. One of the creatures touched the center of its belt, emitting a "thin vapor" that caused the artist to fall dazed onto his back.

In the Florida case, scoutmaster Sonny Desvergers and three of his boy scouts were driving through the woods when they noticed a bright light amidst a nearby palmetto thicket. Desvergers stopped the car and walked into the woods, where he encountered a UFO that hovered directly above him and shot a "small red fireball" down at him, causing him to temporarily lose consciousness.

"As in the Cisco Grove encounter, the witness in this case stated that when the vapor reached him, he couldn't breathe. Neither witness claimed paralysis; they simply 'blacked out' from lack of oxygen," Hanlon wrote.

Shrum did not remain unconsciousness for long, however. "I don't think it [unconsciousness] was very long. I was half-conscious. I could feel myself fall over the bow, and then get right up. I doubt if it was more than a few minutes," he said.

The effort to gas him into unconsciousness continued for hours, forming a long night of terror for Shrum. In a pattern that was repeated a multitude of times throughout the battle, the robot would position itself at the base of his tree and release the white vapor, causing Shrum to pass out for a few moments. Then, he would awake, suffer through a brief spell of the "dry heaves," and resume his fight for survival against the strange entities that were assailing him.

EIGHT:
THE BATTLE BEGINS

It was now between 11 p.m. and midnight. Waking up with the dry heaves after receiving his first dose of the white vapor, Shrum knew that his relaxed, detached observation of the events going on around him was over. War had been declared, and he had been thrust into the middle of a perilous fight. At this point, he made the decision to do all in his power to survive. He switched into "fighting mode," determined to use every means at his disposal to make it back to his home, his wife Judi, and his young daughter Donna.

Unfortunately, Shrum entered his personal "War of the Worlds" armed only with a weapon of the most primitive kind -- his archery equipment. Although human society in 1964 had advanced to the point of nuclear weaponry capable of annihilating most life on Earth, Shrum only had at his disposal a weapon that scientists believe may have been used by early humans as far back as 64,000 years ago. Artifacts appearing to be arrowheads from that time period have been discovered in South Africa.

Interestingly, Shrum's lack of modern weapons such as firearms may actually have worked to his advantage. Other persons who have encountered UFOs often report that firearms they had in their possession did not operate, just as engines and other machinery are said to not function. Arrows shot out of a bow, however, are so "low-tech" that the aliens confronting Shrum may have been completely mystified by them. Some researchers have even argued that because the technology exhibited by UFO occupants is so vastly superior to anything on Earth, a low-tech approach may be the key to winning any confrontation with aliens.

2005 Photo of Shrum Holding the Bow He Used During the UFO Encounter

On the night of September 4, 1964, Shrum had at his disposal a large, 60-pound recurve bow with a 28-inch pull. According to Shrum, when fired at close range, an arrow shot from this bow approximates the velocity of a rifle bullet.

Down below, at the base of the tree, the robot and the two humanoids had once more gathered around. Shrum analyzed his potential targets. The humanoids seemed more likely to be seriously hurt by his arrows. However, the humanoids had made no aggressive moves toward him and appeared to be merely observers. In his mind, Shrum could not justify targeting the humanoids, however much he felt that they shared the blame for the assault on him. Although he was now locked in his very own "War of the Worlds," Shrum did not feel comfortable with inflicting pain and possible death on the creatures that seemed least involved in trying to abduct him.

Sketch Done in 2000 by Shrum Showing Encounter Scene

"I really thought that with an arrow I could have penetrated the [humanoids], but then I figured they'd zap me or kill me for sure, and they weren't really a threat to me... For some reason, I did not want to shoot at them. They weren't causing any problems, and I was afraid of shooting them. Plus, actually the robot was the only one that was creating havoc for me."

He chose to target the robot that was using gas to render him unconscious. Shrum said his decision was reached because the robot "was the only one that was doing anything against me. The other two just stood and looked."

Shrum said, "I tried shooting the robot with my bow…. I just pulled it back as far as I could, and hit him the first time …."

When the first arrow, fired from within twelve feet away, struck the robot in the area of its "chest," Shrum saw a very bright flash of light -- "like a big arc flash."

Illustration by Neil Riebe

"It pushed him back against the rocks about two feet," Shrum said, and after being struck by the arrow, the creature "moved back about ten or twenty feet."

Other than causing a flash and pushing the robot back against the nearby rocks, Shrum's arrow did not seem to have inflicted any actual damage. The shot from the arrow, however, did cause the two humanoids to retreat, about twenty or thirty feet, from the base of the tree to the edge of the nearby brush. "Those others [the humanoids] scattered a little bit. I guess it scared them a little."

Summarizing the effects of his first shot, Shrum said, "I had a 60-pound bow, which is a very high velocity. Seeing how the robot was the only thing that was causing me harm, I shot the chest area. It has the velocity of a rifle at that distance because it [the robot] is only seven or eight feet from me. When I hit the chest, the sparks would fly, like an arc welder, kind of. That robot backed up, and it almost knocked him down. He kind of fell back against the rock. The two [humanoids] at the bottom took off and headed for the brush -- and stood out there about thirty feet from me."

He fired twice more, each shot striking and causing another bright flash and sending the robot reeling back a few steps toward a nearby rock. But, in the end, there seemed to be no appreciable damage, and the fallen robot eventually came back close to the base of the tree.

Now out of arrows, Shrum wondered what the response would be to his counter-assault. He waited. The aliens, who did not seem to be carrying any sort of weapons, did not seem interested in retaliating for his bow and arrow offensive. They did not attempt to fire anything in return, and Shrum at no time saw them produce anything that could be construed to be a weapon.

Shrum took an assessment of what else he might use to attack the strange creatures. He did have in his possession six or seven books of matches, and he immediately thought of using fire to scare the aliens away.

"I always carried all kinds of books of matches with me when I hunted," Shrum said. He remembered that when the robot first appeared on the scene, it had moved over to the remains of one of the fires Shrum had previously lit, and the creature swept the embers from the top of the rock, possibly indicating a fear of fire.

Illustration by Neil Riebe

Hoping to capitalize on this perceived fear, Shrum took an entire book of matches, lit it on fire, and threw it down toward the creatures below. To his amazement, his strategy seemed to work, as both the robot and the two humanoids backed away from the tree. "I lit a book of matches and threw it down, just to see if it would scare them away, and it did. They backed up; so, then I started going crazy with fire."

The next missile prepared by Shrum was his hat, which he set ablaze and dropped down to the base of the tree. "I lit my hat and I guess I had a lot of hair oil on it because it really blazed up when I threw it down, right at the base of the tree, and they backed way up."

Before Shrum started using fire against them, the creatures stood within twelve feet of him. Now, apparently frightened by the burning hat, the creatures moved away to a distance of about 50 or 75 feet from the tree.

At the same time, the mother ship also appeared to move to a higher altitude. "As soon as [the hat] blazed, I noticed that this ship shot way up into the air. I didn't see it go up there. I just looked and it was up there. I could just barely see it then...."

In a different interview, Shrum said, "I glanced over at the ship that was over the canyon -- kind of almost level with me -- and it was almost out of sight -- it looked just like a star -- it moved that fast, just in that second."

As far as the creatures, Shrum said they "stayed a good 50 to 75 feet away," but "as soon as the fire started dying down ... they started coming back."

His next thought was to try to start a brush fire down around the base of the tree. Unfortunately, looking around, he noticed very little brush in the area. "The area is pretty well cleared. It's mostly rock and there are patches of brush; so I tried to start them on fire."

Taking all scraps of paper that he had on his person, he set those ablaze and hurled them down, hoping to start some of the sparse vegetation on fire. "I burned everything I had to burn. My hunting license and everything out of my wallet that would burn ... all the dollar bills that I had, I burned."

When he ran out of paper, he began tearing pieces of cloth from his jacket and setting those on fire. It was a desperate at-tempt to continue frightening the creatures in order to stymie their abduction attempts. "I ripped my camouflage clothing off, and I was burning it," he said. "I just ended up with Levis and T-shirt on and shoes. I burned everything that would burn, and I ended up getting just one little fire started." The momentary flashes of fire were not sufficient, though, to keep the creatures at bay for very long.

"I tied some of my shirt that I ripped up to a compass so that I could hit some brush, because there wasn't any [brush] directly underneath the tree. I caught a little pile of brush on fire. I figured that would bring the cavalry."

Unfortunately, the cavalry never came. Still, the occasional puffs of flame raining down from the tree did serve to temporarily keep the aliens away from his tree. "They stayed back as long as there was fire, a good blaze going. As soon as it died down, they'd come back in."

Having now used up everything he had that was burnable except his shirt, belt, pants, and shoes, Shrum climbed to the top of the tree and tied himself to the trunk using his canteen belt "just in case." Remembering that he would have fallen out of the tree earlier in the encounter if he hadn't been resting on his hunting bow, he decided to lash himself to the tree to secure his position.

"After I moved up to the top of the tree, I took my military belt and moved it out to the last hitch and put it around me and the tree, so that in case I did get gassed, I wouldn't fall down." This simple move turned out to be extremely crucial to his survival on this most frightful of nights.

At some point after securing himself to the tree, Shrum noticed that a second robot had arrived on the scene and was now standing beside the first one. Other than the inconvenience of being put to sleep and then waking up with the dry heaves, Shrum was holding his own against the creatures. However, the aliens' tactics were about to change, and they were about to make a final, determined assault to reach Shrum.

NINE:
FINAL ASSAULT

After Shrum secured himself to the tree, the original robot approached the base of the tree and again emitted the gaseous vapor and again caused Shrum to black out. When he woke up a few minutes later, he discovered the new plan being implemented by the aliens. After the robot had gassed Shrum, the two humanoids started trying to climb up the trunk of the tree in an effort to reach the first limb, which was about twelve feet off the ground.

Shrum had reached the first limb by standing atop a four-foot-high rock located at the base of the tree; however, the humanoids did not attempt to use the rock. Instead, they were trying to boost each other up the trunk in order to attain the limb.

Shrum said, "The two in white tried to boost each other up the tree. Every time they would get up, I just grabbed a hold of the tree and [would] shake it as far as I could, bend the tree as far as I could …. As soon as there would be the least little movement, they'd get down. They were, I guess, uncertain of just what happened, and it kept them down."

In order to encourage the humanoids to remain on the ground, Shrum commenced a strategy of throwing anything he could find down at them. He began by breaking limbs off the tree and using those.

Next, Shrum found coins in his pockets and began hurling them down at the climbers. Although the coins weren't much of a deterrent, they did seem to temporarily grab the aliens' attention. As it turned out, the creatures apparently later gathered the coins up and took them along with them when they left. "Somebody told me later that the coins give dates -- they give pictures -- so maybe that was the reason they got most of the coins." Indeed, to an alien race interested in learning more about a society, few artifacts could offer as much useful information as coins.

NICAP Artist's Rendition of Humanoids
Attempting to Climb the Tree

"Coins are a great spokesperson ... to the archaeology and history," says Grahame Johnston of the Web site *ArchaeologyExpert.co.uk.* "Not only do they provide a real life portrait of famous historical personalities but also the reverse side often reveals daily life at that time. Many ancient coins are stamped with impressions of men plowing, warriors fighting, temple facades, slaves and captives working or bound, and various other activities that provide us with insights into ancient life that otherwise would be lost forever."

Among humans, coins are a fairly recent innovation, having first appeared sometime after 700 B.C. Coins require at least minimal skills in working metal. Coins arise only when a society is advanced enough to organize itself and is economically sophisticated enough to use tokens or symbols in place of items of actual, inherent value, such as gold and other precious metals.

Coins typically contain written communication, including letters and numbers, which are useful in deciphering the society's language. There are instances where coins have assisted linguists to better understand ancient languages.

Coins also contain drawings and sketches of persons and things. Modern-day U.S. coins contain finely detailed sketches of important historical figures, as well as drawings of other important symbols of our societal structure. These would constitute important information for anyone wishing to learn more about us.

The coins Shrum threw at the aliens bore evidence of a fairly advanced technology. They were precisely crafted, delicately engraved, and flawlessly machined. It seems understandable that the coins thrown down at them would make the aliens pause for a few moments, take notice, and later carry the coins away with them.

For Shrum, however, throwing the coins down was an act of sheer desperation. "Anything I had with me I threw down, just to try and distract them. And this went on all night. As soon as the humanoids would leave, the robot would come up to the base of the tree and emit another cloud of vapor."

"I'd be shaking the tree and then this gas would get me, and I'd black out, and then as soon as I'd wake up, I'd heave, and as soon as I'd come to my senses, they'd be just starting to get up the tree."

Apparently the creatures were hoping to nab Shrum before the effects of the gas dissipated, but this was simply not happening. Before the humanoids could climb up to grab him, Shrum would awaken and fight them off. "That's how I knew that I wasn't unconscious for very long, because every time they would gas me, when I woke back up, they'd just be starting to try to climb the tree again."

At one point, when Shrum threw down his canteen, one of the humanoids ran over and picked it up, examined it, and then tossed it aside. "They picked it up, and I guess they didn't want it," Shrum said. "They threw it back down."

Every time Shrum shook the tree, causing the two humanoids to lose their hold and stop climbing, the aliens would retreat to a distance of about 25 feet from the base of the tree. While this was going on, Shrum noticed that other humanoids, possibly three or four more, had arrived on the scene. These others were combing through the surrounding vegetation and seemingly gathering something, perhaps plant samples.

2005 Photo of Canteen Thrown by Shrum during Encounter
(Courtesy of Donald Shrum)

"I could see them going over a rock every once in a while, or hear them out in the brush, thrashing around .... It seemed like they were scouting for something, looking for something. I don't know what .... I'd say there were five or six [humanoids] altogether. I might have seen the same one several times, I don't know."

Getting desperate and running out of objects to throw, Shrum tried some unorthodox battle strategies. "I tried all kinds of goofy things. You know, just tried to distract them. I tried yelling and making all kinds of noises."

Hearing coyotes howling in the distance, Shrum imitated a coyote's call, hoping that the visitors would think that the howling was a signal to unseen allies, requesting reinforcements. "I even howled like a coyote to make these guys think there was more of me coming."

3/27/2000   3/27/2000

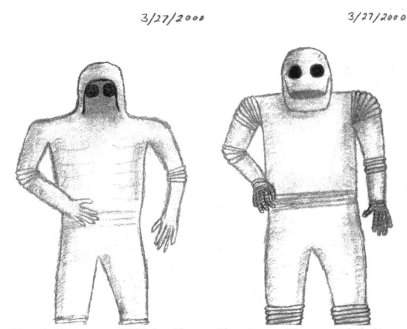

Sketch Drawn in 2000 by Shrum Showing a Humanoid (left) and a Robot (right) -- Courtesy of Donald Shrum

His efforts apparently fell on deaf ears. "They just went around their business like I wasn't there. They didn't seem to hear," he said.

The robot continued to render him unconscious with gas, and the humanoids kept up their attempts to climb up the tree. "It went on all night," Shrum said. "All night long, and that's all that I can remember. Gas would come up, and I'd black out.... I'd be shaking that tree and then this gas would get me, and I'd black out, and then as soon as I wake up, I'd heave … and as soon as I'd come to my senses, they'd be just starting to get up the tree [again]."

Now engaged in a deadly struggle with no end in sight, Shrum grew anxious and depressed. In the solemn desperation of the long night, he even briefly entertained the notion of killing himself by leaping from one of the branches on the other side of the tree that overhung a deep cliff. However, when his situation seemed gloomiest, he thought of his young wife, Judi, and of their one-year-old daughter, both of whom he yearned to hold and kiss again. "When I was up in the top of that tree, I even thought about just jumping off, down the canyon, and killing myself. But the only thing that kept me going is that I had a little girl and my wife. That kept me fighting."

Within him grew a solemn resolve to keep fighting to the end, to resist as long as possible, and to somehow make it back home to his family.

The eastern sky was beginning to show the first pink traces of dawn, and the temperature had fallen to 32 degrees Fahrenheit. Finally, the repetitious cycle of attempts to dislodge Shrum from the tree ended, and something totally new occurred.

The two robots moved close together, facing each other, while standing at the base of Shrum's tree. Peering intently through the tree's branches and sparse leaves, Shrum saw the entire area around the base of the tree bathed by an intense illumination that emanated from both robots.

He watched in fascination as flashes of light moved between the two robots, bursting outward from one and being absorbed by the other, which would then issue a responding burst of light. It was an eerie display indeed.

"They stood facing each other and [it] just looked like a bunch of flashes going between them, like arc flashes … they just lit up the whole area beneath that tree, going back and forth between these two," Shrum said.

Illustration by Neil Riebe

As this dialogue of light continued between the two robots, large volumes of the same strange vapor as before began drifting up toward Shrum's perch in the tree. The rapidly expanding mist became so thick that Shrum could no longer see the robots down below. Suddenly, he felt a blast of intense cold, and once again, he passed out, hanging limply by his belt, which he had fastened to the trunk near the top of the tree. "I blacked out, colder than heck then."

This time, the combined effect of being gassed by both robots apparently caused a prolonged period of unconsciousness. When he passed out, it was still dark, but when he finally awoke, the first rays of the morning sun had appeared, and his long, torturous ordeal was finally over.

Immediately after his experience, Shrum was worried about what might have occurred during his final, extended period of unconsciousness. Did the humanoids successfully climb up the tree and reach him? If they did reach him, what did they do to him? Could he possibly have been taken by them for analysis and experimentation and then later returned to his same location in the pine tree?

Later, after much reflection and after undergoing hypnotic regression, Shrum became convinced that the UFO occupants were never able to reach him at all. "I beat them at their game. I'm one of the ones that got away."

"They probably didn't like me at all. I was a failure to them. I think I was just going to be another specimen," said Shrum, who still believes that he came dangerously close to becoming a victim of alien abduction.

But his apparent success did not come without a cost. The ordeal haunted and consumed him for quite some time. His wife said later, "The first year and a half after his experience Don had terrible nightmares. He would wake up hollering and screaming (and it was frightening to me to hear a man scream because of total fear). On numerous occasions after we'd go to sleep at night and be sound asleep, he would wake up terrified in a cold sweat and holler, 'Those eyes -- those eyes.' That's all I ever heard him say during those nightmares. After he was fully awake, he would tell me he had dreamed about the humanoids and saw their large, dark eyes were staring at him. This would happen again and again."

TEN:
DAYBREAK

Donald Shrum's long ordeal finally came to an end shortly before sunrise on Saturday, September 5, 1964. "I don't know how long I was unconscious. Then when I woke up from that, it was light, but the sun hadn't come up yet. You could see just a dim glow in the sky. I was just hanging by my belt -- my head down and my feet down.... And they [the aliens] were gone. I knew I'd made it. I lived through the night."

In a different interview, Shrum added, "When I woke up, I was hanging just by my belt. My feet were hanging down, and my head was hanging down. It was light, but the sun hadn't come up yet, and there was no sign of them [the aliens]."

The temperature was at freezing and, cold and exhausted, Shrum made his way out of the tree and noticed, on the ground around him, strange small footprints, like those of child wearing moccasins. Also scattered on the ground were all the items he had thrown down earlier, including his canteen and his bow. He recovered his bow, canteen, and two of his arrows, which he found in the nearby bushes. Upon returning to the area about two weeks later, he recovered the third arrow.

The coins he had thrown, however, were nowhere to be found, and Shrum believed the aliens had taken them. "I threw better than a dollar's worth of change down. I don't know if it was bright objects they picked up or not." Shrum theorized that the creatures may have been fascinated by the shininess of the coins and decided to collect them for further study. Or, as mentioned earlier, perhaps the coins were taken because the information engraved on them was useful to their study of the Earth. The other items he threw, however, were essentially ignored.

Illustration by Neil Riebe

Also lying on the ground at the base of Shrum's tree were the remnants of burned clothing and scraps of paper, as well as the small burned patch of brush he had managed to set on fire from up in the tree.

After surveying the scene of his amazing encounter the night before, Shrum walked slowly away from his improvised camp, leaving behind the pine tree that had been his shelter for the past twelve hours.

Shrum headed in the direction of the camp he and the others had established the day before. He walked for about half a mile but then, overcome by fatigue, he lay down on the ground and fell asleep, his nose running due to the cold and his body aching due to the night spent in the tree.

After about five minutes, he was awakened by the sound of someone whistling nearby. It was Vincent Alvarez, who had gone out looking for him. Shrum yelled out to him, and Alvarez found him and helped him to his feet.

"I was the one that found Don as he was heading towards camp," Alvarez wrote later. "The night had been very cold, and all he had [on] at the time I found him was a thin cotton Tee-shirt and his pants. He was weak and exhausted and tired."

Not knowing what had transpired, Alvarez helped his friend to the camp and ministered to him. "I helped him to camp, fixed some soup for him and put him to sleep, he kept on saying that he would have been all right if they had left him alone. I didn't know what he meant, so we let him sleep. He slept for about six hours."

It was clear to Alvarez and Trueblood that Shrum had been through some kind of serious ordeal, although they had not yet heard the full details of his encounter. Even though they did not yet know all that had happened to Shrum, his condition was such that they realized something out of the ordinary had transpired.

Alvarez said, "When he [was] awake, we asked him how he felt, he said fine. Then he said, turn on the radio (we had a small one), there may be something on the news about the space ship that I saw." The men brought out the radio and tuned to a station from Reno, Nevada. According to Alvarez, "The news did say something about a light in the sky."

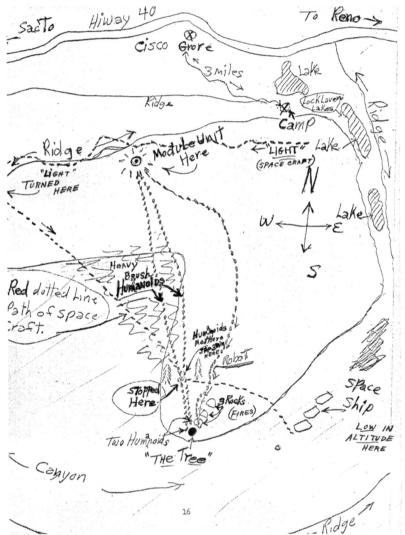

Sketch Drawn by Shrum Showing Where Everything Happened During His UFO Encounter

After having rested, Shrum told his companions what had happened to him. "I told them more of the story, and they be-

80

lieved me. They saw the condition I was in." His fellow hunters listened in stunned silence as Shrum recounted his sighting of the two UFOs and the appearance of the strange creatures that came out of the ships.

Alvarez, who had also briefly lost his way, said that some time after dark, he too had seen what he first thought was a shooting star, but he told Shrum, "I never saw a shooting star come in that low and last that long." He was convinced that his friend was telling the truth, as a result of his own sighting.

Shrum said, "He [Alvarez] said he saw a bright light, kind of like a meteor, but it was going real slow, though. And so I figured that was them [the aliens] coming down from the atmosphere."

When Shrum arrived back at his home in Orangevale, his wife Judi immediately knew that her husband had been through some type of harrowing experience. "The day Don came home from his hunting trip, I knew something was wrong when I saw him," she later wrote in a letter to UFO investigator Paul Cerny. "He was white as a sheet. He was walking as though he had walked for hundreds of miles … His eyes were dazed looking. He spoke to me in a very shaky voice. He had dark circles under his eyes. He looked terrible. His arms were covered with pitch, also his pants and T-shirt. He had small scratches all over his arms."

But Shrum's physical appearance was not as disturbing to her as was his behavior. She remembered, "He came in and didn't even say hi, hello, or anything. He sat down on our couch and said he had something he had to tell me. He then proceeded to tell me about his Cisco Grove experience. His hands shook and his voice was subdued and very shaky. It seems as though he was on the verge of crying. I believe he might have had a slight case of shock."

According to Mrs. Shrum, her husband sat on the sofa and began speaking to her in a very subdued, shaky voice, telling her about his bizarre UFO encounter in the woods near Cisco Grove. "I've got something to tell you," he began. Seeing his demeanor, she became scared and very worried about him. She listened intently as he related his unusual experience. After hearing her husband's story, Mrs. Shrum sought advice from her father, Albert H. Legg, Sr., who had recently retired from the Air Force after thirty years and had been stationed at the nearby Mather Air Force Base. A master sergeant and drill instructor, Legg had been the highest ranking non-commissioned officer and still had connections with the top brass at the base. Legg called his former colleagues and asked if the military had been conducting any kind of maneuvers in the area where Shrum had his encounter. He was told that there had been no maneuvers on the night in question.

Don Shrum (middle) and Don's brother Bill (right),
Two Weeks After the UFO Incident

The encounter affected Shrum so profoundly that he was unable to return to his job at Aerojet right away. He had a runny nose that wouldn't go away and chest pains. Mrs. Shrum said, "He was so badly shaken by all of this that he took a week off from work. He wanted to have a doctor look at him because he said his chest hurt him so bad that it hurt for him to breathe," but he was even more concerned about the prospect of having been exposed to radiation from the UFOs.

Judi Shrum said, "What really scared us was that after he got home, he was sick -- I mean his chest hurt him so bad. It was so bad that I talked to my brother who is a nuclear physicist ... has a PhD in that area ... and I asked him what are the signs of radiation sickness."

Her brother was the late Dr. Gerald Lampson of Berkeley, California, who in 1964 worked as a nuclear physicist for Borg-Warner. According to Judi Shrum, what Dr. Lampson told her was horrifying. "He said 'Don will start breaking out in blisters. Then the hair starts falling out....' So I was terrified."

At that point, Mrs. Shrum tried to find a local facility that would test her husband for radiation poisoning; however, she was unable to find one. The military would not do it because Shrum was a civilian. They recommended that he get tested at a facility in Berkeley; however, that would involve Shrum taking more time off from work and a considerable expense. The Shrums decided to just wait and see if any symptoms developed. "We were scared," Mrs. Shrum said. "So we called our family doctor."

Shrum visited the family doctor, a general practitioner, and underwent a complete physical exam, which, according to his wife, found that there was nothing physically wrong with him. "I went to a doctor in Orangevale, because I had pain in my chest and my nose was just running continuously. Later on, they found I had a cold and my chest was sore from rocking the tree -- it was banging against my chest. He said I had a bruise on my chest."

However, regarding possible exposure to radiation, the doctor told the Shrums that they would just have to wait and see if any symptoms developed. Judi Shrum remembers being terrified during this time. "I was 19 years old. We had a young daughter.

I worried that I would have to watch my husband die slowly of radiation sickness. It was a horrible thing to have to go through. As it turned out, there was no radiation sickness."

While there seemed to be no long-term physical problems, Shrum did experience intense emotional problems for some time following his encounter. For at least a year and a half after the event, Shrum suffered from effects that would likely now be classified as post-traumatic stress disorder.

In a letter to NICAP from October 1973, Judi Shrum revealed important details about how the UFO incident affected her husband long after 1964, "I feel there definitely has been an emotional reaction from Don that this 'Cisco Grove Incident' has been responsible for.... I am concerned because the 'incident' has affected Don.

"The first year and a half after his experience Don had terrible nightmares. He would wake up hollering and screaming (and it was frightening to me to hear a man scream because of total fear). On numerous occasions after we'd go to sleep at night and be sound asleep, he would wake up terrified in a cold sweat and holler, 'Those eyes -- those eyes.' That's all I ever heard him say during those nightmares. After he was fully awake, he would tell me he had dreamed about the humanoids and that those large, dark eyes were staring at him. This would happen again and again; then, they finally stopped.

"One night when we lived in Orangevale in a mobile home on my parents' property, outside the bedroom window was a willow tree that an owl had perched in. The owl started hooting, again we were sound asleep, and Don sat straight up in bed and was completely covered with perspiration and scared because of this hooting noise the owl had made. He made the comment that he thought that it was 'them' coming after him. After these nightmares, it was always very hard for him to go back to sleep again.

"Eventually, the nightmares stopped, but he is still a little frightened; always in the back of his mind is that incident when we go camping or hunting. He was never afraid of the dark or to be out in the woods after dark until that happened. Now when he hunts the evening hunt, he is always back to camp before dark.... I would call that an emotional reaction and he is still that way after nine years since that happened ....

"He started getting a loud buzzing in his ears since a camping trip we took in 1969 to Westwood, California .... Don, I feel, associates this buzzing in the ears with his experience.... I know it sounds crazy or unreal or we're making something out of nothing, but what I don't understand is when he gets this buzzing, he always looks up towards the sky. He tries to hide this from me or pass it off lightly, but I know him. Several nights here in the past year again we've been sleeping and I'll wake up and find Don sitting up in bed with the curtains pulled apart, looking up in the sky. When I ask him what he's doing, he just says his ears were buzzing again."

"We moved to Citrus Heights and by coincidence bought a house that was next door to the home of Vince Alvarez, Don's old hunting buddy. Vince and his family would go camping a lot. Vince was raised in Westwood and worked in the lumber mills up there. So we went up to Westwood on a camping trip with Vince and his family.

"We went about five miles up a dirt road and camped along Duffy Creek, which was a nice place to camp. And that night, Vince and his wife Gloria ... and Don and I were sitting around the campfire, talking, and all of a sudden, I noticed Don got really quiet. He's kind of a quiet person anyway, but I noticed that he got really quiet. Then I saw him turn around and look back behind him up to this ridge -- this mountain ridge that was behind us. Three or four minutes went by ... and here comes this light in the sky, just traveling really fast and very high, and then a few seconds later there was a smaller light right behind it, following in the exact direction and path of the first one, going just as fast. Then we lost sight of them -- they went over a mountain and were gone.

"Later, I asked Don what made him look toward the ridge. He said, 'Well, I got this buzzing in my ears, and I got the sense that they [aliens] are around, or they're going to come after me.'

Later that night, after the campfire was taken care of and Vince and his wife went into their tent, I noticed that Don went and got his handgun, checked to see if it was loaded and put it under his pillow, which Don never did before when we went camping. So, I thought 'This is serious. This really shook him up.'

"Several hours later, in pitch darkness, we could hear noises in our tent ... something was cracking and crunching -- walking around the tent. We didn't get up. We figured it was a deer. The next morning, we got up, packed up, fixed breakfast real quick, and got out of there."

Shrum's UFO experience deeply affected him for the rest of his life. In a 2005 interview with Ruben Uriarte, Shrum said the encounter gave him "a fear of the woods." He told Uriarte, "It has definitely affected me in a lot of ways. Some positive and some negative. I still ... if I'm alone out in the woods, I get kind of panicky. And, as a hunter, it almost completely stopped me from hunting. I only went out a couple of times after that, and I was very uneasy when I was by myself in the woods."

In the years after his experience, Shrum studied other UFO cases similar to his, such as the 1975 abduction of logger Travis Walton from a forest in Arizona. "That Travis Walton movie I saw [*Fire in the Sky*] kind of brings back memories and shows me that they [aliens] are not cute little guys that you can say 'hi' to. Definitely they tried to hurt me."

In the 2005 interview, Shrum stated that the Cisco Grove encounter also affected his two hunting companions, Vincent Alvarez and Tim Trueblood. "It almost ruined them as hunters," he said. "Because every time it would get dark and they'd hear a noise in the woods, they'd panic. So it affected a lot of people"

ELEVEN:
COVER UP

In the days following his UFO encounter, Shrum wanted very much to let people know about what happened to him. However, he hesitated to go public with his encounter for fear of being ridiculed and possibly losing his job. "I was afraid that if it got out, they'd think I was a kook and get rid of me," Shrum said.

Although he felt that he needed to get the story off his chest, he held back from releasing it to the general media. Instead, Shrum and his wife sought to disclose the encounter to certain individuals who might be able to offer help and advice. One of these persons was a retired astronomy professor named Victor W. Killick, who was in charge of the Astronomical Observatory of Sacramento City College.

Shrum's mother in law, Beatrice Legg, came up with the idea of contacting Killick, one of her former professors, and telling him the story, in hopes that Killick could help the family make sense of what had happened that night in the forest. Killick became the first "outside" person to hear of the UFO encounter, and he was also the first "expert" to offer an objective analysis of the case, just days after it had taken place. Killick later wrote, "These people [the Shrum family] all appear in good health and rational. The family believes the man's story.... I have a certain degree of confidence in their veracity and sincerity."

Portion of Letter by Victor W. Killick Regarding the Shrum Case

The story of how the Shrums contacted him was told later by Killick in a letter written on September 9, 1964 to Air Force officials: "During the last 12 years, the writer has had charge of the Astronomical Observatory of Sacramento City College. In the course of our operations, I receive telephone calls and letters from civilians, government officials, and the military seeking identification of sky objects they report having seen. Most of the reported sightings concern astronomical objects, night flying planes, search lights, etc. As yet, I have never had a hoax reported."

Killick continued, "Last Saturday [September 5, 1964] afternoon, a woman, unknown to me, phoned my residence saying she had been referred to me by the *Sacramento Union* [newspaper]. She stated that her son-in-law had seen some strange lights in the sky the previous night while on a hunting trip in the mountains and wanted to know if anyone else had made a report of it. I replied that we had a report of a brilliant meteor having passed over Los Angeles and which had exploded in the Sierra east of Visalia, but that event had occurred on Thursday night.

"I questioned her for details on what her son-in-law had seen, and she called him [Shrum] to the phone. He told me that on Friday [Sept. 4], he and two companions went out for a deer hunt with bows and arrows into the region of the Loch Leven lakes in the vicinity south of Cisco, off Highway 40. During the late afternoon, they separated to hunt. As darkness approached, he realized he was lost and rather than risk trying to find his way back to their camp in the dark over rough terrain, he decided it would be safer to stay where he was until dawn.

"He says he found a tree in a protected location, climbed into it and fastened himself to one of its branches with his belt. Soon he noticed a glowing light moving and hovering along a nearby ridge. He describes it as moving laterally and vertically, over and beyond the ridge. It made no sound. It came closer and at an estimated distance of ½ mile some sort of vehicle appeared to land on the ridge.

"Shortly thereafter he heard a crackling of someone approaching through the nearby shrubbery. Two human beings, about 3-feet tall [Shrum later said they were about 5-feet tall], dressed in white came and stood under his tree and looked up at him. They did not speak but uttered a cooing sound resembling the sound of a dove. Later, two other robot-like moving objects appeared. These emitted a noxious gas which tended to gag and choke him. He shot three arrows at them, one of which hit a robot with a metallic sound and was recovered later. He finally tore off parts of his camouflage suit; set fire to pieces with matches he carried and dropped them to the ground in an effort to start a small grass fire which he hoped would attract the forest service. This caused the visitors to leave him unharmed.

"I ascertained he is a married man, 26 years old, employed at Aerojet plant here. Has a brother also employed at the same plant. His hunting party applied for a fire permit at the nearby ranger station. He stated he knew the story was hard to believe and that he did not want to let it get out in the newspapers, and did not plan to reveal his name, which I did not press him to do, but I did get him to give me his mother-in-law's telephone number. He said he thought it was his duty to notify someone in authority to have the matter investigated (as a public security matter). On September 8th, I received another telephone call from the wife of the man. They made an appointment to meet me

89

at my house and appeared shortly after 1 p.m., together with his brother. They brought along a forest service map, pin-pointed the location [of] the episode and also the arrow in question with a dented point.

"I told them that the Air Force may want to investigate the incident; that I was skeptical myself, but would like to assist in helping them get to the bottom of it. They said they would welcome and give assistance to such an investigation, provided no publicity was attached to it.

"As far as my contact with them goes, these people all appear in good health and rational. The family believes the man's story. They told me that when he got home, he was 'as pale as a sheet' and badly shaken up. I did a little probing to try and find an ulterior motive without success. I have a certain degree of confidence in their veracity and sincerity.

"If you decide to have the matter investigated, I think I can arrange for a private meeting with the principal and his family and your investigators. Yours very truly, Victor W. Killick."

Killick's letter was dated September 9. Interestingly, the letter was addressed to the commander of Mather Air Force Base in Rancho Cordoba, California, but the response to his letter came from McClellan AFB.

Mather Air Force Base was host to the Strategic Air Command's 320th Bombardment Wing, home to a number of B-52 Stratofortress heavy bombers that were maintained on 15-minute alert, fully fueled and armed in case of a Russian attack on the U.S.

McClellan AFB, on the other hand, in 1964 was part of the Air Force Logistics Command, headquartered at Wright-Patterson Field near Dayton, Ohio, whose intelligence division had been studying unidentified flying objects since 1947. The Air Force's official inquiry into the UFO phenomenon began with the establishment of "Project Sign" at Wright Field in July 1947, at the time of the alleged crash of a UFO near Roswell, New Mexico. Project Sign became Project Grudge in 1949 and then Project Blue Book in 1952, all of which were under the jurisdiction of the Air Force Logistics Command, of which

McClellan AFB near Sacramento was a part. It was clear to any-one interested in the UFO issue that Wright-Patterson was the military base with the closest connection to the phenomenon.

*General Exon Shown During His Military Career (left)
and Later in Life (right)*

This division's involvement in UFO research and secrecy is legendary among UFO writers and researchers. A *Wikipedia* article explains, "Wright-Patterson AFB is known among those involved with UFO conspiracy theories as the home of Project Blue Book and because of its connection with the Roswell UFO incident of July 1947. Some believe that Hangar 18, assigned to the Air Force's Foreign Technology Division at Wright-Patterson, along with the Area 51 installation in Nevada, contain, or once contained, wreckage of a crashed UFO."

In 1964, Wright-Patterson AFB was commanded by Brigadier General Arthur E. Exon, who coincidentally, is the highest ranking military officer to ever publically acknowledge that the incident at Roswell definitely involved an extraterrestrial craft.

"They knew they had something new in their hands. The metal and material was unknown to anyone I talked to. Whatever they found, I never heard what the results were. A couple of guys thought it might be Russian, but the overall consensus was that the pieces were from space. Everyone from the White House on down knew that what we had found was not of this world within 24 hours of our finding it," Exon is quoted as saying in the landmark book *Witness to Roswell* by Tom Carey and Don Schmitt, published in 2007.

In the April 25, 1988 issue of *The New Yorker* the late Barry Goldwater, Republican U.S. Senator from Arizona, states that he repeatedly asked his friend, U.S. Air Force General Curtis LeMay, if there was any truth to the rumors that UFO evidence was stored in a secret room at Wright-Patterson AFB. Goldwater also asked LeMay for permission to visit the secret site. Goldwater stated that LeMay became extremely angry, gave him "holy hell," and told him, "Not only can't you get into it but don't you ever mention it to me again."

Thus it was that two U.S. Air Force officers representing the very division that is believe to carry out the military's policy of UFO secrecy, met with the Shrums on Friday, September 25, 1964, just three weeks after Shrum battled the aliens in the Tahoe National Forest. The meeting, which had been arranged by astronomer Victor Killick, took place at a private residence located just outside the Air Force base property.

Judi Shrum said later that the house where the meeting took place was odd and had a cold, lifeless feel to it. She said, "We were taken inside this house. They have off- base housing. What I noticed about this house was that it was very bare. There were no personal items of anyone's ... no pictures or anything. We sat at the kitchen table."

The Air Force officers, a captain and a sergeant, introduced themselves to the Shrums. The captain, a tall, slim black man, was identified years later in Air Force documents as "Captain McCloud," but on the day of the interview, the Shrums both said he claimed his name was "Cloud." Mrs. Shrum remembered thinking it was odd that someone named "Cloud" was assigned to investigate UFOs, which often appear in the clouds.

The other officer, whose name the Shrums did not remember afterward, turned out to be Sergeant Major R. Barnes, according to USAF documents. He was a short, stocky Caucasian with sandy-colored hair.

Mrs. Shrum said, "When Don and I walked in, they walked us in through the living room and into the kitchen. We sat down at the kitchen table. And what I noticed was that it looked like a Hollywood set, because there were no personal items in that house at all. It was bare ... devoid of personality -- most houses have the owner's personality in it. Clearly nobody lived there. It was out of the way, off the beaten path, kind of a hidden setting ... non-descript little box house. The house felt cold ... to me it felt cold -- it wasn't comfortable. It didn't feel like anybody lived there. It was cold and empty."

Illustration by Neil Riebe

Most of the questioning was done by Barnes, who sat at the kitchen table with the Shrums, while McCloud stood off at a distance, listening intently and only occasionally interjecting a question of his own. Barnes recorded the interview on a Wollensak portable reel-to-reel tape recorder.

The officers told the Shrums that they wanted additional information about the sighting that had been reported to them by astronomer Victor Killick. There ensued a two-hour visit regarding the UFO incident, after which, according to Judi Shrum, the officers' report of the interview was submitted to Air Force intelligence at Wright-Patterson Field. She assumed that McCloud and Barnes were attached to that command.

During the course of the discussion, Donald Shrum cooperated fully with the Air Force representatives, despite the fact that they did not seem completely receptive to his story. "The way they asked [questions] was more ... non-believing," Mrs. Shrum said. "I sure thought they should take a neutral stance when questioning people, but, to me, it was like they were talking down to Don."

"They tried to disillusion me in every way they could," Shrum said. Nonetheless, he cooperated fully, and, at one point, showed McCloud and Barnes one of the arrows he fired at the robots during the encounter. The arrowhead had, melted on it, an aluminum-like metal. The tip was bent over on the end, and the metal that seemed to be melted on it appeared to have very muted, rainbow-like coloration.

When the officers asked Shrum if they could take the arrow to have it analyzed for any metal fragments that might have adhered to the tip, Shrum was happy to oblige. "They took the arrow head -- the main one -- and said 'We'll get back to you, and you can have this back as soon as we get through with it' -- which they never did."

Regarding the three arrows he recovered from the scene, Shrum said, "The Air Force got the best one. The point was bent over about 45 degrees, and it looked like it had turned blue from the fire [caused by striking the robot]. It had little light aluminum-like scrapings that were real fine grooved, melted on it when I hit the robot."

The Air Force later claimed that Shrum did not give them the complete arrow -- only the tip, which Shrum strongly disputes, and that no analysis was ever conducted by the Air Force.

In September 1968, Major James H. Aikman of the USAF's Community Relations Division in Washington, DC, wrote a letter in which he stated, "A formal investigation was conducted by McClelland [sp] Air Force Base on September 25, 1964. Mr.

Shrum provided the Air Force with an arrow tip, but not with a complete arrow. The tip was not subjected to any laboratory analysis. It has been loaned to the University of Colorado UFO Study Group, and as yet has not been returned to Mr. Shrum."

DEPARTMENT OF THE AIR FORCE
WASHINGTON 20330

OFFICE OF THE SECRETARY

SEP - 9 1968

Dear Mr. Bloecher:

This replies to your letter of August 28, 1968, in which you requested information concerning a sighting by Donald Shrum on the night of September 11/12, 1964, in the vicinity of Cisco Grove, California.

According to Air Force records, Mr. Shrum experienced his sighting the night of September 5, 1964 (not September 11/12). He reported his sighting to an astronomical observatory. The observatory reported the incident to Mather Air Force Base in a letter dated September 9, 1964.

A formal investigation was conducted by McClelland Air Force Base on September 25, 1964. Mr. Shrum provided the Air Force with an arrow tip, but not with a complete arrow. The tip was not subjected to any laboratory analysis. It has been loaned to the University of Colorado UFO Study Group, and, as yet, has not been returned to Mr. Shrum.

The Air Force evaluation of Mr. Shrum's sighting is carried in the OTHER category.

Sincerely,

JAMES H. AIKMAN
Major, USAF
Chief, Civil Branch
Community Relations Division
Office of Information

Air Force Letter Acknowledging Shrum UFO Case

In addition to turning the arrow over to the two Air Force officers, Shrum gave the men a detailed, annotated map of the area of his sighting, thus providing them with the exact location of the encounter. Shrum became convinced later that the Air Force used this information to send a military team to the location and remove any remaining evidence in an effort to cover up the UFO encounter.

Two or three weeks later, Shrum and his brother Bill, along with friends Vincent Alvarez and Bill McAdams, returned to the scene of the incident, only to discover that unknown persons had combed the entire area, picking up every shred of evidence and raking up the ground to make sure they didn't miss anything and also, possibly, to obliterate the strange footprints that Shrum had seen on the ground following his encounter. In short, Shrum said the area had been "picked clean," and rake marks were very clearly evident.

Shrum said, "When we went back, the area had been raked -- an area of, probably, 50 feet around that tree ... so I know the Air Force checked it out pretty good."

Shrum was able to find, inside a nearby Manzanita bush, the third arrow that he shot at the robot on the night of his encounter. The fact that the arrow was mostly hidden in the bushes would explain why the "cleanup crew" had not found it. "For an inexperienced, non-bow hunter, as most of them probably were, they would not have seen the dark, camouflaged arrow in the brush," Shrum's son, Dan, explains. "To them, the arrow would have looked like the twigs and branches of a typical bush. Only my dad knew exactly where the arrow might be. Only he knew that the arrow had bounced off the left side of the robot's chest and had moved at a 45-degree angle into the nearby bushes."

Other than the arrow, which was mostly hidden in a bush, Shrum found no other physical evidence of his encounter. He said, "This was all the stuff I left there. I know it was there on the morning when I left. I didn't take it back. This stuff was all gone. Nothing. It was cleaned out. They actually raked it -- you could see the rake marks."

What the Shrums and their friends did find was evidence that a large group of men, most likely Air Force personnel, had been at the scene and had meticulously cleaned up the site. They found cigarette butts, discarded cigarette packages ("different brands"), and at least one cigar butt scattered around the area. To this day, Shrum believes the U.S. Air Force hastily put together a task force for the specific purpose of collecting all remaining evidence from Shrum's UFO encounter.

Snapshot of UFO Encounter Area Taken During Revisit
In October 1964

Shrum believes that the Air Force, using the map he gave to Captain McCloud and Sergeant Barnes as a guide, visited the site of the encounter, probably in a helicopter, and cleaned the entire area of any shred of evidence that would tend to corroborate Shrum's story of his encounter with alien beings. "Then I knew the Air Force had been out there for sure and that at least they believed my story," Shrum said.

His brother Bill spoke later with UFO investigators and confirmed the details of the return visit to the scene, as had been reported by Donald. During the visit, the men did find burned spots in the brush around the base of the tree, which obviously happened when Donald threw burning objects down from the tree to try to start a fire.

In addition to making evidence disappear, the Air Force also initiated a disinformation campaign, according to Shrum, that began on the day that he met with the two officers. On that day, Barnes told Shrum that the "aliens" he encountered in the forest might have been a group of "Japanese." Barnes said, "During the war (World War II), we had trouble with the Japanese."

PROJECT 1073 RECORD	
DATE - TIME GROUP September 6 Night	**2. LOCATION** Sacto Area, California
SOURCE Alien	**16. CONCLUSION** Other (PSYCHOLOGICAL)
NUMBER OF OBJECTS Multiple	Encounter with "beings" attributed to psychological causes.
LENGTH OF OBSERVATION 1 Night	**17. BRIEF SUMMARY AND ANALYSIS** SEE CASE FILE. All night encounter with strange beings.
TYPE OF OBSERVATION Ground-Visual	NOTE: Arrow Head and Taped Interview in Specimen File.
COURSE Varied	
PHOTOS Yes No	See Also: Specimen · 7-3745-422
PHYSICAL EVIDENCE Yes No	

FORM
USAF 42 0-329 (TDE) *Previous editions of this form may be used.*

USAF Report Attributed Sighting to "Psychological" Causes

Perhaps after realizing the absurdity of this theory, Barnes suggested another "possibility." He told Shrum that maybe what he encountered in the forest was a group of mischievous teenagers "trying to pull a prank."

The theory about teenagers was also very difficult to swallow because of the isolated location where the UFO encounter took place. "I told them I could just see a bunch of teenagers dressed in space suits way out in the middle of nowhere," Shrum said.

Barnes then took another stab at explaining away the incident. He suggested that a group of Air Force trainees may have been out on "bivouac" in the mountains and could have been responsible for the encounter. However, Shrum's father-in-law had already called the Air Force to find out if there had been any military exercises on the night of the encounter, and he was told that there had been no such exercises.

Shrum also felt that if he had stumbled into the middle of some kind of Air Force training exercise, he would have surely been ordered to leave the area at once. He said, "They'd know some way of getting me out of there if they wanted me out."

In the end, the report submitted to Wright-Patterson by McCloud and Barnes classified the nature of the UFO encounter as "psychological." Entered into the report as a comment was the dismissive statement: "Encounter with 'beings' attributed to psychological causes."

Years later, Shrum admitted that his dealings with the Air Force after his UFO encounter were the absolute worst part of his whole experience, "The fact that they made me out a liar, like I was seeing things, hallucinating…. You don't hallucinate all night long."

There were even hints during the Air Force questioning that Shrum and his hunting buddies might have been drinking on the night of the encounters. Mrs. Shrum said, "They alluded to Don and his buddies drinking in camp. I spoke up and said that Don doesn't drink and neither do his buddies."

The arrow that Shrum gave the Air Force investigators may have been the strongest candidate for metallurgical analysis. Unfortunately, the military made the specimen disappear, claimed they never analyzed it, insisted they no longer had it in 1968, and said they "loaned" it to a "University of Colorado UFO Study Group."

DEPARTMENT OF THE AIR FORCE
WASHINGTON 20330

OFFICE OF THE SECRETARY

OCT 1 1968

Dear Mr. Bloecher:

This replies to your letter of September 12, 1968, in which you requested further information on the S████ report from Cisco Grove, California, in September 1964.

In reply to your first question concerning identification of the Professor of Astronomy concerned, the Air Force does not release the names or addresses of individuals involved in UFO sightings without their permission. This policy must be enforced to protect the individuals concerned from possible embarrassment and undue or unwanted publicity.

In reply to your second question as to the specifics of the "Other" evaluation for this case, it was evaluated as "Other (Psychological).

We hope this information will be of value to you in your search for information concerning this sighting.

Sincerely,

James H. Aikman
JAMES H. AIKMAN
Major, USAF
Chief, Civil Branch
Community Relations Division
Office of Information

Second USAF Letter about Shrum Case

This Colorado group was the Committee of the Scientific Investigation of Unidentified Flying Objects, led by Edward U. Condon, which conducted its study from November 1966 to November 1968. The group was informally known as the "Condon Committee," and its final report was called the "Condon Report."

Funded by the U.S. Air Force, the Condon study was the only major UFO study every undertaken by a public university. Its work and its results were highly controversial and very unsatisfying to many people, including most UFO investigators. The

100

report concluded that science has very little to gain by studying the UFO phenomenon, and many people today believe that the Condon report is one of the key reasons that interest in studying UFOs declined dramatically after the report was issued in 1968.

1964 Photo of Shrum with Young Daughter
(Courtesy of Donald Shrum)

"It kind of totally upsets me when people say that they [extraterrestrials] don't exist ... that they're not out there ... that they're peoples' imagination ..." Shrum said recently. "After going through what I went through, it upsets me that people still think that way. Of course, I was that way before my incident. I never took a personal interest in them [UFOs] before."

TWELVE: INVESTIGATION

Although one arrow was lost to the Air Force, Shrum still had two more of the arrows that he used during the Cisco Grove encounter. He loaned both of those to NICAP investigator Paul Cerny so that a metallurgic analysis could be done on the strange metal flakes that had adhered to both arrow tips. In preparing them for analysis, the arrowheads were pulled off the cedar shafts and packed in cotton inside a box. Unfortunately, as it turned out later, the method used for packing the arrowheads may have contributed to the key trace evidence being lost.

The arrowheads were sent for metallurgic analysis to a laboratory in Pennsylvania that was often used by NICAP for testing UFO evidence. In a letter dated June 13, 1966 to NICAP assistant director Richard Hall, the lab's consulting engineer Henry C. Kawecki wrote, "Dear Mr. Hall -- In reply to your letter of June 3, in reference your November 15 letter together with enclosures, our analytical people could find no trace of any substance on the arrowheads and therefore there was nothing to be analyzed."

This analysis did not fully satisfy Paul Cerny, who wrote in a letter to Richard Hall, "I am sorry that they found nothing of interest in the chemical analysis. When I sent the arrow head in, there was a tiny smear of platinum colored metal on one of the blades of the arrow tip. Possibly this could have worn off or flaked off in transit."

Cerny later explained to the Shrums that the arrowheads were packed in cotton prior to being tested, and by the time they were removed from their packing, the strange traces of metal had flaked off and fallen onto the cotton. The lab accidentally threw away the cotton, along with the metal flakes.

Henry C. Kawecki

Consulting Engineer

Box 151

Fleetwood, Pa.

Tel: (A.C. 215)
WH-4-8080

June 13, 1966

Mr. Richard Hall
Assistant Director
National Investigations Committee
on Aerial Phenomena
Washington 6, D. C.

Dear Mr. Hall:

In reply to your letter of June 3, in reference your November 15 letter together with enclosures, our analytical people could find no trace of any substance on the arrowheads and therefore there was really nothing to be analyzed.

Best regards.

Sincerely,

Report on Chemical Analysis

Later, Kawecki wrote to Cerny, "I am returning herewith at the request of Mr. Richard Hall of NICAP, the arrowheads which you had submitted for analysis. As he has probably informed you, we were unable to find material for analysis other than the steel of which the arrowheads were made. Your story's a very interesting one, and I regret that we could not be of help. Yours very truly, Henry C. Kawecki."

One of Shrum's arrowheads somehow ended up in the possession of UFO researcher Dr. J. Allen Hynek, and after Dr.

Hynek passed away, it was reportedly donated to University of Arizona. It is not clear if this arrowhead was the one taken by the Air Force or one of the two loaned to NICAP.

Henry C. Kawecki

Consulting Engineer
Box 151
Fleetwood, Pa

Tel A '15
W H 4 8080

October 28, 1966

Mr. Paul Cerny
Box 2132
Sunnyvale, California

Dear Mr. Cerny:

I am returning herewith at the request of Mr. Richard Hall of NICAP, the arrowheads which you had submitted for analysis.

As he has probably informed you, we were unable to find material for analysis other than the steel of which the arrowheads were made. Your story's a very interesting one and I regret that we could not be of help.

Yours very truly,

Second Letter Regarding Arrowhead Analysis

The other arrow lent to NICAP was returned to the Shrums, but they later lost it while moving to a new house. The arrow taken by the Air Force, which Shrum believes was the best specimen of the three, remains unaccounted for.

"To this day my mother and father have not received the arrow back from the USAF," Dan Shrum said. "My father and mother have told me, though, that they would like it back. The USAF promised they would return dad's arrow to him. It's been far too long and overdue."

Cover of True Magazine, Jan. 1965

In the year following the Cisco Grove encounter, the Shrums became increasingly frustrated by the "UFO ignorance" they encountered around them. Finally, in January 1965, four months after the encounter, the Shrums picked up a copy of *True* magazine, which featured a story called "U.S. Air Force Censorship of the UFO Sightings," by Major Donald Keyhoe, co-founder of the National Investigations Committee on Aerial Phenomena (NICAP). They were so inspired by the article that Mrs. Shrum wrote a letter to him, as follows:

MAY 26, 1965 LETTER FROM JUDI SHRUM
TO DONALD KEYHOE

Major Keyhoe,
My husband and I read your article in *True* magazine (Jan. 1965) and was very pleased to learn of your organization

[NICAP]. My husband had a very weird experience with an UFO and its inhabitants in September of 1964 while hunting for deer with two other men off highway 40 at Cisco Grove in California. This area is known as Desolation Valley. His experience is similar to the one of the longshoreman Mr. John F. Reeves in Brookeville, Florida. My husband's experience, though, was with two robots and five short, stocky men with light-colored uniforms.

He had gotten separated from his hunting party and was forced to spend the night in a tree. His experience had started two hours after dusk and ended approximately one hour before sunrise the next morning.

He saw a light off in the distance and thought it might be a helicopter searching for him. He had three signal fires lit on a rock below the tree. This attracted their attention. But when it hovered without making a sound, he panicked and climbed up the tree. There is a lot more to his experience than I can put in this letter, because it's so long.

My husband is not one to tell stories, as many people can testify to.

We went to the Air Force hoping they could ease our minds, but they only seemed to laugh it off and say he had hallucinations, until they sensed he was very serious about the matter.

Among other things, Don had even shot several arrows at one of the robots. The next day, he had picked them up. We gave one to the Air Force to make a metallurgy test on it, and they kept it and have never returned it or have given word on what they found. When I saw the arrowhead, it had grayish scrapes on it, which was caused by hitting the robot. The Air Force also made a tape recording of Don's story and told us they would send us a copy reel, which they never did.

The reason we have waited so long to write is because we've been hoping to hear from the Air Force but never have.

I wrote you because we hope we can help you further your investigation on UFOs.

We have succeeded so far in keeping the story out of the newspapers because of public ignorance on the subject of UFOs.

The United Press from the Pentagon tried to reach us, also our local paper (*The Sacramento Bee*). My husband works for the missile industry and is afraid of ridicule and possible loss of job.

Don & Judi Shrum, Circa 1975

A month later my husband and some other people went back to the area and took some pictures.

If you are interested in the complete story, please contact us … Orangevale is in Sacramento County and about six miles from Folsom, California.

And if you are not interested, please just disregard this letter.

[End of Judi Shrum's letter]

This letter to Keyhoe launched the NICAP investigation spearheaded by Paul Cerny. In mid-1965, Cerny began a long relationship with the Shrums in an effort to get their story out in a proper manner without revealing their identities. Cerny, assisted by fellow NICAP member David Slette, conducted an exhaustive interview of Shrum in July of 1965 (see Appendix A for full transcript), which is the key investigative document in this case, along with Cerny's NICAP report (see Appendix B).

1978 Photo of Shrum (left) with Paul Cerny (right)

In Cerny's initial notes about Donald Shrum, he wrote, "Is an average quiet young man, interested in hunting, sports, and racing cars. He is quite shy, doesn't want publicity of any kind, and doesn't want to become known publicly in connection with the experience. He is a typical hard-working family man, has an attractive wife and child, is extremely sincere and honest."

Cerny's notes continued, "He came very close to completing graduation from high school but dropped out shortly before. He has since taken extra training courses and classes, particularly in helix-arc welding. He is steady, reliable, and calm, has a great job, and has a nice home and car."

Unfortunately, his "great job" vaporized two years after his UFO encounter, when Shrum, his brother Bill, and fellow hunters Vincent Alvarez and Tim Trueblood were laid off by Aerojet General, along with numerous other workers. Shrum believes that the layoffs were due to Aerojet losing a large government contract and does not think it was related to his UFO incident. "Only my immediate family, Vince and Tim knew about it," Shrum said. "Everyone else just didn't know, and I never talked about it."

Then again, the U.S. Air Force had an extensive file on Shrum and his UFO encounter at its intelligence division at Wright-Patterson Air Base. Since Aerojet made missiles for the Air Force, it is highly likely that the upper management of the missile company *did* know all about Shrum's encounter. Nonetheless, it remains uncertain where this was a factor in the dismissal of Shrum and his hunting companions from Aerojet.

One month after leaving the missile company, Shrum took a job as a truck driver and warehouse worker with Heieck Supply of Sacramento. He loaded and delivered plumbing equipment for residential and commercial customers. Shrum worked with Heieck for 32 years, until his retirement. Though he settled into a comfortable routine, he never forgot his strange experience.

As the years passed, the Cisco Grove UFO encounter remained a deep and puzzling mystery to everyone who knew about the case. "There is absolutely no doubt in my mind that this incident is factual and authentic," Paul Cerny wrote many years later. "I have spent considerable time plus many visits with the main witness, and along with the testimony of the other witnesses, I can rule out any possibility of a hoax."

Through the remainder of the 20th century, the Shrums continued to insist that their names not be used whenever the Cisco Grove UFO encounter story was told. They remained very private people and were uninterested in any media attention or public scrutiny. Among the many notable researchers who looked into the case were Dr. J. Allen Hynek, Stanton Friedman, Dr. Anita Uhl Brothers, and Dr. James Harder -- all of whom found it highly credible and worthy of further consideration.

Shrum's encounter was mentioned (without using his name) in a number of magazine and journal articles -- the first to do so being an account published in the July-August 1966 issue of *The APRO Bulletin*, a newsletter of the civilian UFO group called the Aerial Phenomena Research Organization. APRO, which existed from 1952 to 1988 and was based in Tucson, Arizona, was founded by Jim and Coral Lorenzen.

Shrum was contacted in the fall of 1965 by Dr. James A. Harder, professor of civil and hydraulic engineering at the University of California at Berkeley, who requested to interview him and who agreed to pay his way to Berkeley for the session. Shrum, whose case was already being investigated by NICAP, didn't realize that Dr. Harder, a noted UFO researcher in the 1960s, represented APRO, which was a rival of NICAP.

California Man Is Beseiged By 'Occupants'

In early September, 1963, three men from the Sacramento area of California went into the mountains near Cisco Grove, Calif., to hunt with bows and arrows. On the night of the 4th, after hunting a ridge, they separated and headed for camp. One of the men, who will be referred to hereafter as Mr. X (at his request), came to the end of the ridge, found a sheer drop and had to retrace his steps and attempt to descend to camp along another route. At that time it was getting dark and Mr. X shortly found that he was lost.

Excerpt from APRO Bulletin Article

The Shrums later said that they did authorize Dr. Harder to publish a story about the case; however, he never told them that it would be published by APRO. They assumed that Harder was affiliated with NICAP.

Cover of Saga Magazine -- February 1967

The story as published in *The APRO Bulletin* was full of inaccuracies, including the date of the incident, which was given as 1963. The Shrums were dumbfounded as to how so many errors could have crept into the story. The article said that the mother ship "landed," that the robots "floated" rather than walked, and that the humanoids had shaken the tree to make Shrum fall from it -- none of which was true.

Renowned paranormal writer John A. Keel, best known for his book *The Mothman Prophecies*, wrote an article called "UFO Kidnappers" for the February 1967 edition of *Saga* magazine. It retold the Shrum case based on the story from *The APRO Bulletin* article and included the article's inaccuracies.

Keel also added a few misstatements of his own. He said that Shrum was "a U.S. government scientist," which was not true, and that Shrum had been "carefully investigated by scientists from the University of California," which wasn't entirely correct. The "investigation" by Harder and colleague Anita Brothers was rather cursory.

Coral Lorenzen, who founded *APRO* along with her husband, wrote a book in 1967 called *Flying Saucer Occupants*, which contained a lengthy mention of the Shrum case, calling it "the most spectacular report we have examined." The section of the book dealing with the case was basically just an expansion of the article from *The APRO Bulletin*, although it omitted most of the errors and inaccuracies that appeared in the periodical.

In the summer of 1974, Cerny arranged for Shrum to undergo regressive hypnotherapy in an attempt to probe more deeply into the UFO encounter. Paul Cerny arranged to bring a hypnotherapist to the Shrum residence. The doctor, whose name is not recorded in the case documents, arrived at their home and proceeded to induce hypnosis, according to Judi Shrum.

"The hypnotist regressed Don back to about five years old, got him a pad and pen, and asked Don to draw some pictures.... About 25 minutes into the hypnosis session, he ... brought him forward and then forward some more ... childhood memories of certain incidents. Then he brought him forward up to the Cisco Grove incident....

"Then the doctor told Don that he was going to be an observer of the incident and that he wasn't going to be *in* the incident. He would be standing back watching himself and what was going on....

"In about ten minutes when the first two humanoids appeared, walking up to the bottom of the tree, Don's voice started getting agitated. He was getting upset and a little stressed. So I

112

motioned to Paul [Cerny] to have the hypnotist stop. So they did. The hypnotist calmed Don down and re-emphasized that he was just an observer -- not physically going through this. So it calmed Don down and then they were able to go on with the hypnosis session.

Shrum said, "When I was hypnotized, the guy would say 'Go back' and he put me in the tree and through the whole thing, and I started panicking. Judi recognized it and said 'Hold off.' So he brought me out of it a little bit and said 'You'll see it as if you're watching it on television.'

"Now what came out of that hypnosis session -- what I found really interesting -- was, up to that point, Don described the great big craft [mother ship] with the little light in front and three stepped down panels on the side of it, but past that, he didn't quite remember the size of it. Well, under hypnosis, Don said it was a cigar shape and *very large*.

"Another thing that came out was that after it was over, Don climbed down out of the tree .... They asked Don, 'Were there footprints that you saw on the ground?' and Don said, 'Yes, there were footprints.' And the hypnotist said, 'Can you describe them?' And Don said, 'The footprints would be like you'd be wearing a moccasin ... no tread ... small ... but like you'd be wearing a moccasin. Small footprints -- like children's footprints. And that surprised me."

Cerny later wrote in a letter to Shrum, "We were pretty well convinced after the last session that you were not taken aboard the craft as we thought might have been the case." It is apparent from Cerny's comment that he and fellow investigators still had suspicions ten years after the incident that Shrum had actually been taken by the aliens during the encounter, examined on board their ship, and later returned to the pine tree. However, the hypnotic regression conducted in 1974 seemed to dispel this notion. It supported the notion that Shrum was never carried away from the tree by the aliens.

Shrum later admitted to feeling greatly relieved to know, once and for all, that he had, at no point, been actually abducted by the strange creatures that persecuted him back in September of 1964. As it turned out, what he remembered about the encounter was basically all there was to it. He had indeed fought off the aliens and frustrated their attempts to abduct him.

Regarding the hypnosis that his dad underwent in 1974, Shrum's son, Dan, said in a 2011 letter to Ruben Uriarte, "Unlike other abductees that had to undergo hypnosis to remember what happened to them, my father remembers the incident, fully aware, even to this day. Hypnosis was only used to bring out details missed while he was awake and fully aware."

MUFON MUTUAL UFO NETWORK, INC.

THE SCIENTIFIC INVESTIGATION OF UNIDENTIFIED FLYING OBJECTS

September 22, 1974

Mr. & Mrs. Donald R. Shrum
6186 Butler Road
Penryn, Calif. 95663

Dear Don and Judy:

Sorry I have been so long getting a note off to you fine people. My workload here seems to pile up deeper and deeper. Before I forget, I would appreciate you passing on your phone number to me which I do not have. If I cannot stop, I can at least call you when I am near your area.

We gave considerable thought to making another call on you for another hypnosis session, but the distances are great as you well know, plus arranging an agreeable time is awkward. We were pretty well convinced after the last session that you were not taken aboard the craft as we thought might have been the case. We would still be interested in any more associated experiences of possible recurrence, side effects, or camping reminders that you may experience.

Sincerely,

Paul Cerny

Paul Cerny

1974 Letter Regarding Hypnosis Session

As the decade of the 70s moved along, network television took a stab at telling the Shrum story. In 1978, an episode of the Jack Webb-produced NBC television series called *Project UFO* (also known as *Project Blue Book*) featured a story that was very loosely based on the Cisco Grove incident. It was done without the Shrums' permission or involvement.

"The story was done poorly," Judi Shrum said. "Of course names were not used and things were changed in the story, probably to avoid a lawsuit. Every time this is done in books or articles by UFO researchers they change Don's experience which makes it appear as if he is the liar when in actuality the writer is covering their own butt at his expense. I know this sounds harsh, but it has been our experience."

After 1978, the story lay dormant for a number of years. It was mentioned again in the 1988 book *Uninvited Guests: A Documented History of UFO Sightings, Alien Encounters and Cover-ups*, written by Richard Hall, one of the original NICAP investigators.

The case resurfaced in 1995, when original investigator Paul Cerny teamed with Ted Bloecher to write an article called "The Cisco Grove Bow and Arrow Case of 1964." The story, which was based almost entirely on Cerny's original NICAP report (see Appendix B), appeared in the winter 1995 edition of the *International UFO Reporter*, a publication of the Center for UFO Studies (CUFOS).

The case was next featured in Preston Dennett's 2004 book *UFOs Over California*, in which Shrum's name is given as "Donald Smythe" in order to protect his identity. The Dennett book caused a revival of interest in the case, and shortly thereafter, the Shrums decided to stop withholding their true identity.

Donald Shrum's identity was fully revealed in print for the first time in 2007, when the story of his encounter appeared, along with his name, in an article titled "The Cisco Bow and Arrow Alien Encounter" by Steven Reichmuth, in the April 2007 issue of the *MUFON UFO Journal*.

After decades of trying to stay "below the radar" with their UFO story, Donald and Judi Shrum finally broke the long silence about their encounter at a 2005 MUFON chapter meeting in San Jose, California, at which author Ruben Uriarte was present. For the first time, they consented to have their identities revealed in connection with the Cisco Grove case. It was on that night that the seeds were sown that eventually led to the publication of this book.

At the MUFON meeting, even though it had been 41 years since the UFO incident, Shrum still seemed uneasy and uncomfortable in discussing his strange experience. The Shrums displayed the 60-pound hunting bow and the water canteen that Donald carried with him on the night of the encounter. The canteen, which appeared to be a typical World War II item in a cloth pouch with belt hook, was the one Shrum threw at the aliens. Shrum did some repair work on it after the UFO incident, though, because the canteen was punctured when it struck a jagged boulder.

Shrum holds the 60 lb. bow that he carried on the night of the UFO encounter in this year 2005 photo.

Shrum also displayed an arrowhead similar to those used the night of the encounter. All of the original arrowheads have, unfortunately, gone missing over the years.

In telling his story again after so many years, Shrum admitted for the first time the depth of despair that he experienced during the long siege by the aliens. He admitted having thoughts of suicide when there seemed no hope of escape. A part of the tree that he had climbed overhung a deep cliff, and he thought about leaping to his death below. Although these dark thoughts intruded into his consciousness, his will to survive and fight to the end won out.

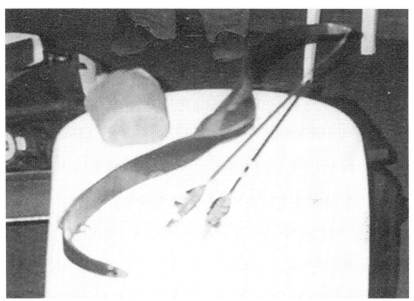

Display Showing Canteen, Bow, and Arrows

In 2007, the Shrums contacted authors Ruben Uriarte and Noe Torres, requesting that they serve as the custodians of their story for future generations. Knowing the Shrums to be gentle, kind-hearted, and trustworthy souls, the authors agreed. The authors promised that they would work to put together a book about this amazing story. The Shrums gave Ruben all their photographs and documents on the case, and Ruben was also able to obtain all the files collected by Paul Cerny about the incident. The result is the book you now hold in your hands. It is a long-overdue telling of what really happened to Donald Shrum on the night of September 4, 1964 near Cisco Grove, California.

Asked what the experience means to him so many years after the fact, Shrum replied during a 2005 interview, "Well, I found out that they [extraterrestrials] do exist, no matter what anybody said. "From what I experienced, UFOs are real."

Does the encounter so many years ago still affect him? "It's not something that's eating at me all the time, but certain things come up or certain things I see take me back to it. It is something that I will probably never get over."

He is convinced beyond a doubt that the creatures he encountered were not of the Earth, and he believes, based on the behavior he observed, that they were on some kind of scientific mission to our planet. Would he want to ever meet them again? Hesitating a bit, he replied, "Only if they were in a cage."

AFTERWORD
By Ruben Uriarte

In 2005, my good friend and fellow UFO researcher, Noe Torres, approached me about working with him on a book called *Mexico's Roswell* regarding a reported mid-air collision between a small plane and a UFO along the Texas-Mexican border in 1974. The book turned out to be a success for us, and it resulted in a number of media appearances, including an episode of the History Channel's *UFO Hunters* series.

After *Mexico's Roswell*, we looked into a number of other reported crash retrieval cases that occurred in years past in the southwestern United States. As our research unfolded, we began seeing recurring patterns in the eyewitness testimonies regarding these UFO incidents. Most notably, we saw similarities in how the various government and military agencies reacted to each event. Invariably, these agencies tended to deliberately distort the facts and hide evidence from the general public.

As this "official" obstruction of truth has continued unabated to the present day, we became convinced that the best UFO evidence may be gained by studying historical cases from the 1940s, 1950s, and 1960s -- before the "iron curtain" of UFO secrecy was put completely into place. The tactics for keeping UFO evidence away from the masses have become so sophisticated in our day that studying the historical cases may actually be the closest to the truth that we can get.

Almost since the first wave of UFO sightings occurred in the 1940s, official procedures have been in place to cover these incidents up, recover evidence, bully witnesses, and discredit testimony. Early government agencies, including *Operation Blue Fly* and *Project Moon Dust*, were reportedly given the task of retrieving trace evidence of UFO encounters and keeping UFO information hidden from the public.

The origins of these policies may be traced back to the historic 1947 UFO crash near Roswell, New Mexico. After rancher Mack Brazil told military officials that he found a huge area of metallic debris from a crashed UFO at his ranch, the Army immediately acted to secure the location. Military personnel reportedly went to the Foster Ranch and carefully collected all evidence from every square inch of the crash site. Witnesses said that soldiers combed the entire area on their hands and knees to ensure that nothing was missed.

Along with the clean-up of evidence in Roswell, witnesses were bullied, threatened, and harassed into never revealing what they had seen. Although many witnesses did eventually speak out, many years later, a large number have chosen to heed the warnings they were given immediately after the incident.

Many UFO researchers believe that the Roswell UFO cover-up became the "blueprint" by which other UFO incidents were later kept hidden from the public. Roswell set the pattern, and the same tactics have been employed ever since.

A similar cover-up occurred following the reported crash of a UFO in 1955 near Del Rio, Texas, as told in our book *The Other Roswell: UFO Crash on the Texas Mexican Border*. The book recounts the story of the UFO encountered by Air Force Reserve pilot Robert B. Willingham while flying his F-86 jet fighter on an escort mission for a group of B-47 bombers over West Texas. He saw the object speed past him at over 2,000 miles per hour before it rapidly lost altitude and crashed near the Rio Grande River, just south of Langtry Texas. Willingham returned to the impact site later that same day in a small plane and landed it near the crashed saucer. He found Mexican Army soldiers guarding the wreckage and awaiting the arrival of the "American Air Force."

When Willingham flew over the crash site two weeks later, he observed that the impact site had been completely cleaned of any evidence. It looked like soldiers had gone over the large stretch of desert "with a fine tooth comb." Then, Willingham received a series of threatening phone calls from officers attached to military intelligence advising him never to speak about what happened "down on the border" or there would be severe consequences.

Then, in 1964, after the Cisco Grove UFO encounter in Northern California, Air Force investigators dispatched out of Wright-Patterson Air Base interrogated eyewitness Donald Shrum. After he told them the exact location of his encounter, the area where the incident happened was completely cleaned of all evidence by "unknown individuals." Upon returning to the scene a couple of weeks later, Shrum found that the ground had been "raked" and all remaining traces of his UFO encounter had been completely obliterated. Shrum also found evidence, such as cigarette butts and empty cigarette packs, to indicate that a large task force of men had scoured the area in an apparent UFO clean-up detail.

Meanwhile, the Air Force interrogators from Wright- Patterson tried to convince Shrum that what he had seen in the forest had been either a group of renegade "Japanese" left over from World War II, some military personnel out on maneuvers, or perhaps teenagers engaging in a prank. These "explanations" were clearly part of the attempted cover-up.

We are very fortunate to obtain the full permission and co-operation of Donald Shrum and his family in telling, for the first time ever in book form, this amazing story of a very brave man who survived a hard-fought encounter with forces completely unknown to our planet.

My involvement with this case began when I was the assistant director for the Mutual UFO Network (MUFON) of Northern California in the late 1990s. I acquired an old case file with notes and documents about the Shrum case that had been compiled primarily in the 1960s by the National Investigations Committee on Aerial Phenomena (NICAP).

The chief investigator in the Shrum case was Mr. Paul Cerny, who had been with NICAP and then joined MUFON and became director of MUFON for Northern California. Having known him personally, I can say that Cerny was an outstanding investigator and researcher who dedicated much of his life to investigating the UFO phenomenon in a consistent and logical manner. Cerny left his post as director of Northern California to become MUFON's Western Regional Director, and Mr. Virgil Staff took over as Northern California director. I served as Mr. Staff's assistant director, which is when I first became acquainted with the Shrum file.

After Mr. Cerny's unfortunate passing on November 27, 2000, Virgil Staff replaced him as Western Regional Director, and I became MUFON's director for Northern California.

I reviewed Cerny's files on Donald Shrum's incredible UFO encounter near Cisco Grove, California, and found it to be one of the most spectacular and believable UFO cases I had ever heard of. After reading the documents and notes, I was totally amazed at this man's courage and will to survive in a 12-hour struggle to keep from being abducted by the strange beings he saw coming out of a UFO.

I also found to my surprise that, unlike other abduction stories where the details are revealed only after the witness undergoes hypnosis, Donald Shrum was fully conscious and aware of everything going on around him for most of his UFO experience, except for several instances when he was briefly knocked out by a strange gas that was used against him by the beings.

When I first learned about this case, I did not know the witness' true identity, because his real name had never been given out publically by Paul Cerny and the other original investigators. They had used aliases in order to protect Mr. Shrum. I became so interested in this case that I made up my mind to one day meet this brave man who had faced up to a most bizarre and unearthly threat and had overcome it. It was a fascination that I could not shake.

I finally had the good fortune to meet this amazing person and his family in September 2005, thanks to my former MUFON colleague, Kathlyn Bunyard, who introduced me to Donald Shrum, his wife Judi, and their son Dan. The Shrums invited me to stay at their home for several days as their guest, during which time I was able to conduct in-depth interviews with both Donald and Judi. For the first time, I heard the intriguing, heart-pounding story of Donald's encounter with the aliens in its entirety and directly from the eyewitness himself. As I listened intently, Donald and Judi gave a full account of the incredible experience that had occurred 41 years nearly to the day of the interview. As I continued listening, I reflected on how it must have felt for Paul Cerny when he first heard this breathtaking testimony.

As the interview continued, I carefully observed and studied Don's expressions as he recounted his incredible tale of outwitting the aliens and avoiding capture. I could see on Don's face that he was still very troubled by this frightful experience even after so many years had elapsed. I was also very interested in Don's description of the two distinctly-different creatures he observed -- the "humanoids" and the "robots." The term "robot" is not used too often in eyewitness descriptions of UFO occupants, although many of these strange beings do appear to possibly be androids, robots, or other forms of automatons. As our own society continues to rely more and more on robotic automation, why wouldn't these strange visitors to the Earth use similar technology?

During my interview with the Shrums in 2005, Donald showed me the 60-pound bow with which he fired at the aliens and the water canteen that he threw down at them. One of the humanoids picked up the canteen, examined it carefully, and then threw it back down, seemingly uninterested. Holding that very same canteen in my own hand, I was struck by the realization that it had previously been touched by a being from another world. I wondered what the visitors' agenda had been. Had they specifically targeted Mr. Shrum for abduction or was he just a chance specimen that wandered across their path? Had they previously abducted other humans?

In 1964, Donald Shrum experienced his very own "War of the Worlds," utilizing the most primitive of tools to battle a foe whose technology was obviously far beyond Earth's. During his encounter, Shrum used a pine tree for cover, used man's most primitive ally -- fire -- to keep the aliens at bay, used simple weaponry -- a bow and arrow -- to stymie the opponents, and, in the end, his low-tech resistance against a technologically superior foe proved successful. Whereas the aliens might have been able to prevent guns from firing and may have been able to cause other kinds of electromagnetic disruptions, the visitors apparently had no answer for the basic force of fire and the simplicity of bow and arrows.

After spending much time researching this case and talking to the Shrums, I totally believe that Donald's heroic experience is completely true and fully authentic. I completely endorse it as a factual, believable, true event.

And, the thing that stuck with me the most about Donald's description of what he went through during that desperate struggle for survival in a dark California forest in 1964 were the words Mr. Shrum used to conclude our interview with him....

"I won," he said. "They didn't take me."

Ruben Uriarte, October 31, 2011
Union City, California

APPENDIX A:
ORIGINAL INTERVIEW

What follows is an interview from July 10-11, 1965, nearly one year after the UFO encounter, conducted by NICAP investigators Paul C. Cerny and David Slette. The text of the interview is based on a transcript prepared from the original audiotapes. No content has been changed. We have made some corrections for grammar and have removed extraneous pauses and spaces that were originally transcribed along with Shrum's words. It's important to note that, as he thought further about the case and later underwent hypnotic regression, some of the details became clearer, and certain parts of the story changed a bit.

NICAP: And you had this experience near Cisco Grove on Highway 40 and do you remember the date now?
SHRUM: The sixth and seventh of last September. [The actual date was September 4 & 5].

NICAP: Then that was almost a year ago now?
SHRUM: Yes.

NICAP: Now, what were you doing out there and who were you with?
SHRUM: I was with two other fellows. I was bow hunting.
NICAP: This was before rifle season?

SHRUM: This was before rifle season. And we packed back in, and I got separated from the rest of the party.

November 21, 1968

Mr. Ted Bloecher
% NICAP
1536 Connecticut Avenue, N.W.
Washington, D. C. 20036

Dear Mr. Bloecher:

Your recent letter to the Director, regarding the opening date of our 1964 archery deer season, has been referred to our Branch for reply.

The archery deer season in the Cisco Grove area opened on August 29, 1964 (Saturday) preceding the Labor Day weekend which was within the legal open season. The season closed on September 13, 1964 (Friday).

If we can be of further assistance, please contact us again.

Sincerely,

E. C. Fullerton, Chief
Wildlife Protection Branch

Letter from California Fish and Game Department Confirming Dates for Hunting Season in 1964

NICAP: How did you happen to do this?
SHRUM: We hunted all day Friday, and we just got too far out. I was the farthest out.

NICAP: You actually more or less separate and fan out?
SHRUM: Yes.

NICAP: Did you have walkie-talkies or anything?
SHRUM: No. We kept each other in sight up to that one point. I was on top of this ridge and the other fellows were down below and they told me to go on around, and they didn't realize it was as far around as it was. By the time I got around ... my sense of direction isn't too good -- I just go by the sun and it was going down.

NICAP: And they wanted you to take a long hike?
SHRUM: Yeah. I got down in this real brushy country. I couldn't tell. I really got tangled up, and by the time I got out of there it was dark and I could see these rocks up on the ridge -- pretty bright.

NICAP: So you just climbed up there?
SHRUM: So I just got to the highest point to see if I could see the camp and the other fellow... was close enough that one guy was almost right at camp and the other guy was close enough that he saw the lantern from camp so he made it back. And I was just too far out. I was over about three mountains from camp; so, I didn't see it at all. And there was a -- you know -- I planned to spend the night in a tree, so I just got up there. I guess it was maybe an hour passed, and I saw a light; first it was down below the horizon.

NICAP: Was this after dusk? Or after it got dark out?
SHRUM: Yes, it was dark. Just before the moon. The moon was just starting to come up.

NICAP: Was it a full moon or not?
SHRUM: Geez, I can't remember. It was awful bright.

NICAP: Probably close to a full moon?

127

SHRUM: Yeah. And this -- I saw a light, you know, and it looked just like a flashlight or a lantern, at first, bobbing up and down but it was below the horizon.

NICAP: Down below the tree level?
SHRUM: Yeah, below the tree level. I saw it go up over a tree and then down and I thought maybe it's a helicopter from the ranger station.

NICAP: All you could see was just the light; no other object or ship or anything?
SHRUM: That's all I could see.

NICAP: No blobs back of it or anything?
SHRUM: No. It was dark against the hill and that was all I could see.

NICAP: Just the light?
SHRUM: Yeah.

NICAP: White?
SHRUM: Yeah. Not like a beam. It was just like -- you know….

NICAP: A white lamp bulb?
SHRUM: Yeah. Only it didn't show any light, you know.

NICAP: It didn't radiate then?
SHRUM: Yeah. Right. It didn't flash a beam upward.

NICAP: It wasn't really too bright?
SHRUM: Yeah. Right. And it went along this long ridge. It was way back in here somewhere, so I jumped down and I lit three fires on the rocks about ten feet apart just to….

NICAP: Attract their attention?

SHRUM: Yeah. And I stood between two of them and started waving my arms, and they turned and came right up. Oh, I guess within 50 - 60 yards, something like that.

NICAP: Could you see any shape then?
SHRUM: And at this point I still couldn't see any shape. All I could see was this light that it came right up ... was between these two trees and....

NICAP: Did you hear any noise?
SHRUM: That's what scared me. I didn't hear any noise at all.

NICAP: No noise at all?
SHRUM: No, nothing. Just completely quiet and just, you know, hung there, and I was pretty sure it was no helicopter, and at that time all I could see was that little light. I thought maybe it was just a little dinky thing, because I couldn't see anything behind it.

NICAP: What do you think it was that you saw?
SHRUM: Well, I thought of a flying saucer then, but I thought it was just a little tiny one, you know, and, after, so I just threw my bow up in the tree and got up there. And I had camouflage clothing on from head to toe -- all the way -- hat and everything.

NICAP: By the time it got up to you, how far from you do you figure it was in yards or feet?
SHRUM: I say 50 or 60 yards and it ... and after I got in the tree, I just froze -- just sat as quiet as I could -- maybe -- you know -- thought maybe they couldn't see me, because it was dark in the tree ... and it made about a half circle around me and got over this canyon, and the moon showed on it. Then I could see, and then it really scared me. I could see these three -- oh, I don't know -- all I could see was just one surface. It just looked kind of flat to me from where I was.

NICAP: Well, flat. How? This side?
SHRUM: Well, up, you know. And there were just three and …
and they were graduated an even distance apart.

NICAP: Can you draw a sketch of what you shot when you saw?
SHRUM: Yes. Do you want me to draw it later? Anyway, there
were just the three surfaces, and they were all like you would
take aluminum foil and shake it -- you know -- wiggle it against
the fires and would just -- and you could see it glistening effect.
And then this light was way out in front of it. I couldn't see any
attachment to any of them and it just looked like it was out by
itself.

NICAP: Just the one light? And three surfaces?
SHRUM: Yeah. And these three shiny surfaces. And they
weren't too -- they were almost straight out from me, but they
were over the canyon, and they were up a little bit -- and -- and I
set there and watched it -- it must be four or five minutes or so,
and   then something came out of the second one, and all I
could see was kind of a flash. Something went straight down the
hill.

NICAP: Something dropped out?
SHRUM: Yeah.

*NICAP: Was this light just sort of suspended out in front and
forward?*
SHRUM: Yeah. It looked like it was just suspended out there
and ….

NICAP: Far away from the others?
SHRUM: Yeah. Almost like an electric eye or something like
this -- you know. And I saw something come out of the center
one and go straight down the canyon and couldn't see it. It was
dark down there. And I didn't bother much about it -- just kept
my eyes on the other one.

ALIENS IN THE FOREST

NICAP: You couldn't tell what it was or what shape it had?
SHRUM: Unh, unh [No]. And then I heard a kind of a thrashing in the brush up here behind me, you know, coming through the brush, and it was up on the hillside and then I saw this little blinking light, and I could see just a -- and I could see just a -- just like part of a dome on top and just a little light flashing on it. And then I heard all this crashing through the brush down the mountainside and then....

NICAP: Was this on the opposite side then of the canyon?
SHRUM: Yes. This was on the complete -- see, I was right on the point of the canyon, right on the point, and from here to the tree it goes right straight down into the canyon. I was more or less out on the point, and I guess this object went down behind me on the other side but then -- oh I guess five minutes of that crashing through the brush and I saw this first -- uh -- what you call it –person or it was -- a -- some kind of a guy just all in some kind of a light-colored silver or whitish-looking uniform, with a -- you know -- the kind of puffs around sleeves and joints -- and ...

NICAP: Something like our astronauts' suits? Sort of a strain and relief suit?
SHRUM: Yes. And then on the head -- I couldn't see it -- they had a helmet on -- all could see was just a dark face, and it was -- a -- it came within I guess -- oh, a hundred feet, I guess -- stopped and messing around with the Manzanita and stuff, and I don't know what it was doing -- looking or what it was doing. And then it was joined by another one just like it, and they came down right below the tree at the base of the tree and was looking up at me. And it had real large eyes -- eyes as big as silver dollars.

NICAP: How far away were you then?
SHRUM: I imagine about 12 feet -- just right straight down on the tree.

131

NICAP: Any noise or sound come from out of them or around them?
SHRUM: No, just their walking. Oh, they had a kind of -- I guess it was them -- a signal setup affair -- this here kind of a cooing noise -- something like an owl or something would make -- you know -- and I heard it from them up on the hill and -- and from the main ship, I guess. And every time this noise would come from the ship or something, they would do something else --you know -- I just connected it -- it might just have been some owls out someplace, but I connected it -- I don't know. Anyway the two come up, and then I heard this other crashing around me all just over a little bit where they were and I saw these big eyes coming just like two flashlights hooked together or something.

NICAP: Were the eyes illuminated?
SHRUM: Yes. They were -- uh -- just like a candle in a -- just like you put a candle in a flashlight; almost like fire.

NICAP: What color was it?
SHRUM: Oh, just the color of fire. That's what it looked like. And when it come down -- right down the ridge instead of up the canyon like they did -- and it stopped right on top of the rocks, just out in front of me.

NICAP: Just this other one?
SHRUM: Yes. And you could see its head kind of illuminated up real bright because of the eyes.

NICAP: You thought that the eyes were sort of giving off some sort of illumination or luminescence or something?
SHRUM: Well, I don't know. It just looked like fire, you know, just like its head was full of fire, and that's the only way I can explain it.

NICAP: Just what did these things look like? Were they human in form: two legs, two arms, and so on?

SHRUM: Yeah. They were human in form and they just –they seemed awfully short, you know, short, stocky ….

NICAP: Short legs?
SHRUM: Yeah.

NICAP: Short arms?
SHRUM: No, they -- in proportion, they looked like a short man, you know. They weren't too ….

NICAP: Approximately how high would you estimate?
SHRUM: Oh, five foot or so, five foot two or something like that -- not very tall.

NICAP: What about the -- any type of muscular appearance or muscles?
SHRUM: Yeah. They were more or less short and stocky built - you know what I mean?

NICAP: Did all of them look similar as far as their garb and what not was concerned?
SHRUM: The ones in white did. This robot looking affair was a little different. The one with the eyes

NICAP: Glowed or lit up?
SHRUM: Glowed, yes.

NICAP: Did the other that you figured were human, did their eyes glower?
SHRUM: No. It was the ….

NICAP: It was the robot that you signaled -- the robot?
SHRUM: Yes.

NICAP: Was it any different looking in appearance from the others?
SHRUM: Well ….

NICAP: It was the same general build?
SHRUM: It was the same general shape -- a little bit taller --
seems like it was a little bit taller. It was standing up on the
rocks so -where they were standing down below me and it's kind
of hard to get a depth perception.

NICAP: Did you notice any particular features about their feet?
SHRUM: No.

*NICAP: You said they were standing on a rock -- did it have ac-
tual feet or shoes?*
SHRUM: Well, I couldn't see that. I couldn't see that clear, but I
knew it was some kind of metal when I --later on -- anyway, I --
it seemed -- uh -- it could've --the fires I had built were just kind
of cold then, and it took its arm and went through them ashes,
you know, and scattered them all over the place and -- uh -- it
just -- uh, then it came right up right under the tree just where I
got up in the tree and stood there for a while. The others were
still down the base.

NICAP: They were all just watching for that one?
SHRUM: Yes, just looking.

NICAP: Staring?
SHRUM: Staring. They weren't doing anything else. And the
way I was sitting in the tree -- kind of astraddle of one limb
(there was two limbs come out on both sides of me and the bow
stretched across them and resting on the limbs).

NICAP: Did you have any other weapons?
SHRUM: No. That's all you're allowed. You can't have any
firearms.

NICAP: Sidearms?
SHRUM: No, you can't carry them in bow season, and so this --
call it a robot -- and after it stood for awhile, it took … it put one

hand up to its mouth -- I don't know why... and some kind of like a white vapor came out and ....

NICAP: Did it actually have a mouth and facial features, or somewhat?
SHRUM: Like a -- you know ....

NICAP: A Charlie McCarthy type face?
SHRUM: Something like that. Just a hinged jaw or something, but you could see its head looked metal or dark gray of some kind and -- uh -- the way it walked and everything wasn't -- you know -- wasn't flexible like -- like the other ones.

NICAP: How about the body shape of these robots: what did they look like? Were they fashioned just exactly as the beings themselves?
SHRUM: Well, general shape, I couldn't see in detail. The general shape was like a man. And then land this robot, when it kind of white vapor, smoke or whatever it was came out, then I blacked out.

NICAP: It got to you?
SHRUM: Yeah.

NICAP: Did it blow it right at you or something?
SHRUM: Well, it was almost like -- it was a little breeze. He was upwind from me so it just kind of came up through the trees and it act like nitrogen would; just like take the place of air, couldn't breathe, just gas.

NICAP: A stuffy feeling?
SHRUM: Yeah, just gasp for breath and ....

NICAP: Did you notice any particular odor or anything like smog?
SHRUM: No, I didn't. I never did smell anything. There was no smell of any kind, but I just kind of gasped for breath and then I

just blacked out and I fell across my bow and that was the only thing that kept me in the tree and when I woke up I had the dry heaves and then -- uh I figured they were out to get me then. I was going to be peaceful and quiet before that.

NICAP: How long do you feel you were out? Do you have any idea?
SHRUM: I don't think it was very long. I was half conscious. I could feel myself fall over the bow and then get right up. I wasn't -- I doubt if I was out more than ….

NICAP: A few minutes?
SHRUM: Yeah. Two minutes.

NICAP: You were still down in the respective same place?
SHRUM: Yes. And then, I lit a book of matches. I had about six or seven books of matches with me so I lit a book of matches and threw it down just to see if it would scare them away -- and it did. They backed up and, so then I started going crazy with fire then. I lit my hat, and I guess had a lot of hair oil on it 'cause it really blazed up when I threw it down right at the base of the tree, and they backed way up. They stayed away a good fifty to seventy-five feet away and as soon as this blazed, I noticed this ship just shot way up in the air 'cause I didn't see it go up there -- I just looked, and it was just way up there. I could just barely see it then.

NICAP: As you threw the fire down?
SHRUM: Yeah. I guess, I guess it was kind of uncertain itself. And it backed up.

NICAP: And it hung up higher in the sky?
SHRUM: Yeah. It just stayed up higher. I could just make it out up there. If ... And just -- as soon as the fire started dying down, why, they started coming back and you can tell by this terrain in these pictures that there is very little

brush or anything around, and I was trying to catch it on fire, you know.

NICAP: Just about put the tree on fire?
SHRUM: Yeah.

NICAP: That would have been a hot one.
SHRUM: [Laughter] Yeah. The area is pretty well cleared. It's mostly rock and there is patches of brush; so, I tried to start them on fire. Oh, I took everything out of my pockets that weighed anything, and I ripped my camouflage clothing off and -- and I was burning it -- throwing it down -- I hadn't -- oh, I just ended up with Levis and T-shirt on and shoes. Besides, I burned everything I had to burn. My hunting license and everything out of my wallet that would burn, and then I ended up getting just one little fire started. With all that burning and stuff ... But they stayed back as long as there was fire -- a good blaze going. As soon as it died down, they'd come back in.

NICAP: What time of night was this by the way?
SHRUM: Oh, geez, I'd say it was an hour -- two hours after the moon -- I'm not sure -- 12 -1 o'clock... in that area. I didn't have a watch with me.

NICAP: Had you noticed the position of the moon in the sky at that time?
SHRUM: No, I didn't.

NICAP: Backing up a little. You say that when you first noticed this light and you climbed into the tree this was about an hour or two after dark.
SHRUM: Just about two hours after dark.

NICAP: And this was in September?
SHRUM: Yeah.

NICAP: So it got dark about 7 o'clock in September. So about 12 or 1 o' clock would have been a period of about 5 hours - 6 hours.

NICAP: Actually in September I think it would be more like 7:30 or 8 o'clock.

NICAP: Possibly. But then you know it gets dark in about an hour.

SHRUM: It was probably a good three hours after dark.

NICAP: That was when you first noticed the lights?

SHRUM: Yes. I imagine it was around then.

NICAP: Then the whole episode kept on for about how long would you say?

SHRUM: Well.

NICAP: From the time you first saw the light until the time the things went away and left you alone.

SHRUM: Well, it was early morning by the time after, well, after burning everything I could burn I tried shooting the robot with my bow and he was the only one that was doing anything against me. The other two just stood and looked. So, the bow I've got, it's -- it has the velocity of a rifle at that close range -- 12 feet or so. So I just pulled it back as far as I could, and I hit him the first time and it shoved him back against the rocks. But that's all and ….

NICAP: Did it move him?

SHRUM: Yeah. It moved him back and it just -- when it hit it was just like a big arc flash and it just flashed up real bright and I only had three arrows with me so -- so that's all I shot. I hit him three times and all three times it pushed him back a little bit. And just a big bright flash. And I didn't have it all.

NICAP: Approximately where you hit him was on a shoulder somewhere?

SHRUM: Well, it was in the general vicinity of the heart. That's the way I aimed so; so it seemed to push him in that direction. He was right up against the rocks so it didn't· push very far and every time I shot, too, these others scattered a little bit and I guess it kinda . . .

NICAP: Scared them away?
SHRUM: Scared them a little bit. And -- a -- then after I got rid of that I . . . went to the top of the tree and I hung -- I tied my belt around me and the top of the tree just in case.

NICAP: Did they make any attempt to fire anything back at you or anything?
SHRUM: No. There was nothing.

NICAP: There was no return fire.
SHRUM: No return fire or anything.

NICAP: How many attempts were there with this gas?
SHRUM: It -- it went on all night -- all night long that's all I can remember. Well, I don't think I was out more than -- it couldn't be a few minutes -- they would -- these two would try to get up the tree.

NICAP: Oh, they would?
SHRUM: Two in white and tried to boost each other up the tree which is I guess about 12 feet to the first limb from where they were standing. And every time they would get up, I just grabbed a hold of the tree and shake as far as I could bend the tree as far as I could and the tree just as soon as there would be the least little movement they'd get down. They were, I guess, uncertain of just what happened. And it kept them down, and I broke limbs off and threw them down and I threw all the change I had in my pockets. I threw that down and anything I had with me I threw down just to try to distract them. And, oh, this went on almost all night. Just ... gas would come up, and I'd black out and the -- how I timed myself when I was out -- I'd be shaking that tree

and then this gas would get me, and I'd black out, and then … as soon as I … wake up I'd heave and -- and as soon as I'd come to my senses, they'd be just starting to get up the tree so I knew I wasn't out very long 'cause they -- you know they -- I don't think they'd stay away that long, but….

NICAP: Kind of a nightmare, wasn't it?
SHRUM: Sure was. And I tried all kinds of goofy things, you know, just tried to distract them.

NICAP: Yelling or anything like that?
SHRUM: Yeah. I tried yelling and making all kinds of noises. I heard a bunch of coyotes off in the distance howling; so I even tried to do that just to make them think there was more of me, you know, coming, and I tried everything I could think of, you know, to try and distract them. But they just went around there business like -- you know I wasn't there.

NICAP: They didn't seem to hear you at all, huh?
SHRUM: They didn't seem to hear … when I would shout these two -- uh -- in human form would look up and all I could see was kind of a black flat looking face with big eyes.

NICAP: What color were their eyes?
SHRUM: I couldn't tell the color. They were lighter that I could see -- their eyes.

NICAP: They were regular size you would say?
SHRUM: Yeah. Extra. Seems like extra large. And -- uh -- their face was just kind of black looking, and I couldn't see if they had a helmet on or not. And they had white -- I could see the top -- you know-- it looked like a suit they had on and over their head all I could see was a black patch of the face and the eyes. I couldn't make out any features of the face and -

NICAP: Did you notice any kind of a nose?

SHRUM: No.

NICAP: A kind of a funny peaked nose or anything like that?
SHRUM: Well, it seemed like it was awful low on their face.

NICAP: Low?
SHRUM: Low. And flat.

NICAP: Sort of like a banana nose.
SHRUM: Yeah. As well as I could see. It's not too bright in moonlight. You can't see in detail.

NICAP: No?
SHRUM: No.

SHRUM: Oh, the next morning. Oh, well, during the night, too, I could see there must have been I guess five or six of the ones in white all together that I seen. I could see them out, oh, going over a rock every once in a while or hear them out in the brush thrashing around.

NICAP: These three stayed there below the tree about all night so you could -
SHRUM: But these three stayed there -- stayed there all the time, but I could see these others. They just. It seemed like they were scouting for something -- looking around for something. I don't know what.

NICAP: How many was there all together?
SHRUM: I'd say -- oh -- five or six all together. 1 could re-member -- I might have seen the same one several times. I don't know. But, I'd say around five or six. But, uh, close where I -- uh -- I can't tell the time but it was -- you know -- the sky turns pink just before it gets light. It was still dark but the sky was getting kinda -- you know -- getting a little color to it and then this -- uh -- the second robot came

141

down. And they were right -- they moved some rock right to the base of the tree.

NICAP: Moved the rock?
SHRUM: Yes.

NICAP: How big was the rock?
SHRUM: Well, they didn't move it. They just moved from the rock. This other one moved from the rock and -- and they were both below the tree where the other two in white stood before. And they stood facing each other. You can see this tree is pretty skimpy. You can see down through it. And, anyway, they stood facing each other and just looked like a bunch of flashes going between them like arc flashes and all kinds of -- they just lit up the whole area beneath the tree, and they was going back and forth between these two and then the fog just started pouring up, and then I couldn't see 'em after this smoke or whatever it was started pouring up, and it just -- and I blacked out ... colder than heck then. Then, when I woke up, I was hanging just on my belt. My feet were hanging down and my head was hanging down.

NICAP: But still in the same position in the tree though?
SHRUM: Yeah. I was still in the top and my belt was holding me up then and the sky -- it was light, but the sun hadn't come up yet, and there was no sign of them. I don't know, just like that.

NICAP: Now, going back to the ship itself. Did you?
SHRUM: What?

NICAP: You said there was an object that dropped from another object in the sky. Now where did you -- could you see this object on the ground where it was?
SHRUM: Well, all I could see was the top and it was a light of flashing light on the top.

NICAP: The object that dropped out of the ship, you mean?

SHRUM: Yeah. Well, I guess that's what it was 'cause that's the direction they came from. I just....

NICAP: How far was that away? Was there anything associated with it?
SHRUM: It was on this ridge -- this ridge that -- right up here behind me.

NICAP: Down the trail?
SHRUM: This area, yes, right. And this -- oh, right about -- it would be back in here in the picture. It was just on this side of that tree. There's that point. There's a fault like a -- there's a fairly clear up in there lot -- quite a few clearings.

NICAP: Did this thing just float down out of the atmosphere or did it drop down pretty fast?
SHRUM: It went pretty fast. I saw a big flash of light, you know, as it left. I could just see -- I couldn't tell what shape it was or anything. I just see a dark object shoot right straight down, and there was a flash when it came out of the second one, and then I never saw it any more until I saw the light up on the hill. I just figured that was it.

NICAP: Did this ship stay relatively the same distance away most of the time?
SHRUM: Oh, after the fire, it stayed up real high and I never did see it -- you know, it never did come down close again.

NICAP: Oh, it just stayed up there?
SHRUM: It stayed up to the high point, but it was visible all night.

NICAP: Could you still see it on?
SHRUM: I was pretty busy on the ground, and I didn't look up too often.

143

NICAP: How many robots? Was there anything else besides the eyes and the -- this flashing of the arrows that you got off to tell if there was any difference like they were wearing some kind of a garment like the robot?

SHRUM: Well, it was on this rock; it was in the shadow of the tree as far as the moon, and they stand up, you know, and all could see -- I could see the face fairly plain because of the eyes lighting up, and then I seen that one hand when it was going through the fire like it was in joints, but it was like a hand, you know, fingers and everything as well as I could see. I couldn't see much detail from the neck down. It was just a general shape, that's all.

NICAP: Did you notice them carrying anything? Like any weapons or any objects?
SHRUM: No, they didn't seem to have anything.

NICAP: Just walking around barehanded?
SHRUM: At one time when I threw my canteen down, this one from the tree ran over and picked it up and looked it over and threw it back and discarded it.

NICAP: Do you have that canteen yet?
SHRUM: Yeah. It's out in the garage of my father-in-law's. When I came down the next morning, too, all the -- I never found any change. I threw better than a dollar's worth of change down. I don't know if it was bright object that they picked up or what. I never -- it might have lain in cracks. I never --

NICAP: Did you find any of it?
SHRUM: I didn't stay around too long to check. I didn't see too much. I -- I just picked up my bow and I found that one arrow that it was -- I guess after it hit -- it landed in the top of some Manzanita, and of course that's the only reason I found it.

NICAP: Are these the two other fellows that were with you?
SHRUM: No. Let's see -- this is one.

NICAP: This one?
SHRUM: Yeah. This one. This is a later trip. I went out just with my brother.

NICAP: Who were the fellows that were with you?
SHRUM: [omitted] was one.

NICAP: Do you care if I take their names down?
SHRUM: Yeah. I guess it's all right.
NICAP: [omitted] too?
SHRUM: [omitted]

NICAP: Now where does he [Vincent Alvarez] live?
SHRUM: He lives in Citrus Heights. I'm not sure. I don't know the address.

NICAP: You got his telephone number or anything?
SHRUM: Yes, I think I can get that.
NICAP: Does he [Alvarez] work at Aerojet?
SHRUM: Yes. Uh huh. And the other one was [Tim Trueblood].

NICAP: Where does he live?
SHRUM: He lives in Loomis.

NICAP: Probably get those. Probably talk with them. We may like to just call them and talk to them.
SHRUM: Well, now, this …. He was the one in the middle that -- you know -- he was actually lost the same as I was, but -- but … he made it back to camp. He was close enough that he made it to camp.

NICAP: What happened to [omitted]? Did he camp somewhere?

145

SHRUM: Well, he -- he planned on camping out and he stayed out for -- he just got down behind some big rocks and lit himself a little tiny fire -- I don't think he ever did lit -- That 's right. He stayed there for awhile and then he saw [omitted]'s light from camp; so he went on.

NICAP: He went on just for that?
SHRUM: He was close enough so that he could make it on in. But .... He was telling me the next day that he saw this -- uh -- he got -- he thought it was a shooting star at the time, and it stuck out in his mind that he said, "Geez, I never saw a shooting star come in that low and last that long." And that's what he really, you know, he was pretty confident that I was telling the truth after that 'cause he -- you know -- when he saw that. And then we heard a report the next morning on radio out in Nevada that a large meteor was seen coming in the sky which I knew it wasn't.

NICAP: Well, it could have been another meteor, too.
SHRUM: It could have been. But the one I saw wasn't. Well, now the Air Force they tried to tell me that ....

[At this point, Mrs. Shrum mentions that her mother knows a retired Astronomy professor who taught at Sacramento State University and that Mr. Shrum had spoken to him.]

NICAP: He's an Astronomy teacher at Sac State?
SHRUM: He was, but he's retired. But   he's still active in organizations of astronomy.

NICAP: Did you tell him the whole story as you're telling us?
SHRUM: Yes. He is the one that got in touch with the Air Force.

NICAP: He is the one that got in touch with the Air Force first?
SHRUM: He is the one that arranged the interview and all.

NICAP: Did he have confidence in your story?

SHRUM: No, I don't think he did. He kept telling me the instance where his family saw this and that, and it turned out to be searchlights in the cloud or something like that you know.

NICAP: What did he say about these little fellows you were arguing with?
SHRUM: Well, I ….

NICAP: Did he figure this was just a bad dream or something?
SHRUM: He and the Air Force both they tried to say, well, hallucinations…. I told them that hallucinations don't last all night long. And then they tried to say, well, then, you know, during the war we had trouble with Japanese coming over, and then they were trying to say it was teenagers trying to pull a prank, and I told them I could see a bunch of teenagers dressed in space suits.

Mrs. Shrum: And they tried to say it was a group of their trainees out up in the mountains.

Mr. Shrum: And we called the Air Force, you know, later, just to find out if they had any, you know, groups in that area. They said they had no training in the area like that, you know, so, we disproved that. And the fact that they [the aliens] didn't know how to climb a tree or they seemed afraid of the tree and later afraid of fire …. I knew right there it wasn't Japanese or any – you know -- anybody on earth that could cause any common sense would -- you know …

NICAP: They would know how to climb a tree.
SHRUM: Yeah. And they'd know some way of getting me out of there if they wanted me out. I don't know.

NICAP: Now, what about -- you say Captain [McCloud] interviewed you in your home along with the Sergeant?
SHRUM: Yes.

NICAP: They taped the whole interview, and you went up there later on, you said?
SHRUM: Yes. I went there in the rifle season which was ....

NICAP: Did you have anybody with you then?
A· It was my brother and the fellows that I went up with before.

NICAP: And what did you, notice about the particular area where you were at?
SHRUM: Well, it was a desolate area and that's what why it stuck out so much, and it was quite a burned area around there. A lot more than I thought it was when I left.

NICAP: You said that it looked like it was pretty well raked up around the ....
SHRUM: It was raked over and there was quite a different brands of cigarettes laying around, cigar butts, and -- and the area was clean. I had several -- oh like the canteen belt -- there was a lot of metal objects on it and -- uh ....

NICAP: This was something you left there?
SHRUM: This was all stuff I left there. I knew it was there in the morning when I left.

NICAP: You didn't take it back?
SHRUM: I didn't take it back. This stuff was all gone. Nothing. It was cleaned out.

NICAP: Did you see any place where they could possibly set down a helicopter -- the Army or the Air Force?
SHRUM: Well, they could have set down almost any place.

NICAP: Then, the Air Force went down there and really combed over the whole thing?
SHRUM: Yeah. They had a good map of the area there that the ranger station put out, and I had it marked and then plus this area -- it was burnt -- was kind of bright orange looking,

you know. A light color. And it really stuck out 'cause we, when we went back -- we could see the area from quite a ways, you know, when we went down in there.

NICAP: Did you have any of these pictures the time you talked to them?
SHRUM: No, I didn't.
NICAP: Did you show them any?
SHRUM: No, I didn't have. I took these later. But the area would have been easy to find by air with that map. The location from the highway with the lake and the position of the lakes --

NICAP: And the lone tree sticking up there?
SHRUM: Yeah. And the tree out by itself so -

NICAP: Can you tell us anything more about the Air Force action on this particular thing?
SHRUM: They took the arrow ....

NICAP: They took the arrow and never returned it?
SHRUM: They told me they would return it as soon as they checked to see if there were any metal filings on it.

NICAP: Didn't you say that someone said they were going to give you a copy of the tape, too?
SHRUM: Yeah. They said they'd give me a copy of the tape and they also said they'd keep it quiet about my name, but then we got letters from news reporters -- they got information from the Pentagon.

NICAP: Oh, really?
SHRUM: Some reporter came all the way out here. He looked -- he thought that if was Orange -- he heard that it was Orangeville, but he thought it was Orange County all the way down to Los Angeles -- Orange County there -- and it was from International United Press. And he came up here and he looked up --

149

all he knew was that it was [omitted] that lived in Orange and had something to do -- you know -- with UFO. So ....

NICAP: Did you ever talk to him?
SHRUM: No. He -- my brother lives right in Orangeville and he's a [omitted] .... so he said are you the [omitted] that -- you know -- had something to do with UFOs? And they said, no, that's my brother and they said they wanted my number and -- and they told him that I wasn't interested in giving -- you know -- any information to the press, so ....

NICAP: Then you never did directly contact the press?
SHRUM: No, I never did. I got several letters from publishing companies.

NICAP: Did you?
SHRUM: And different news men and stuff, but -- you know -- I just discarded them in the wastebasket.

NICAP: Did you ever inquire about these arrows and try to get them back?
SHRUM: No. I never did try to call back to find out.

APPENDIX B: CERNY REPORT

Note: This is the original written report prepared for NICAP by Paul Cerny on September 25, 1968. The names of the witnesses, which were omitted in the original report, have been added back in the text below. A few of the details as reported by Cerny in this narrative were inaccurate and were later corrected. Also, the witness remembered more as time went on.

On Friday, September 4, 1964, Donald Shrum, a 28-year-old [age was actually 26] factory worker who lived in the Sacramento, California, area, made arrangements to go bow and arrow hunting with two companions -- Tim. R. Trueblood of Loomis, and Vincent Alvarez, of Citrus Heights. On that day, the three men set up their camp in the Cisco Grove area of Placer County, about three miles south of Route 40, near the Loch Leven lakes. They spent the remainder of the day hunting for deer, and, by evening, had become separated. Mr. Shrum found himself at the top of a ridge that ended in a steep drop and found that he had to retrace his path and go around it in order to meet the others. Their camp was about three mountain ridges away. However, this ridge was longer than Shrum had realized, and he missed his companions and lost his way. By this time, the sun had gone down, and as it was getting dark, he decided he would climb the ridge and spend the night in a tree for protection.

151

About two hours passed when Shrum noticed a light below the top of the mountains of the ridge to the north. The moon was just rising, according to the witness. (The moon, just two days prior to a new moon, actually rose on September 4 at 3:30 a.m.) The light, which was moving in a westerly direction in a somewhat zigzag path, "looked just like a flashlight, or a lantern at first, bobbin up and down," according to the witness, "but it was below the horizon .... I saw it go up over a tree and then down, and I thought maybe it's a helicopter from the ranger station." The light was all that Shrum could see; it was white and did not flash or radiate beams as it moved along below the northern ridge.

Mr. Shrum climbed out of the tree and lit three fires on three large rocks below the tree, each about ten feet apart, to attract attention. He stood between two of the fires and waved his arms, and the light suddenly turned and closed in from the northwest to a distance he estimated to be about 50 or 60 yards, at an elevation slightly above eye level. He could see no shape at

"That's what scared me," he told UFO investigator Paul Cerny. "I didn't hear any noise at all. The light hovered between two trees and "just hung there, and I was pretty sure it was no helicopter, and at that time all I could see was that little light. I thought maybe it was just a little dinky thing because I couldn't see anything behind it. I thought of a flying saucer then, but I thought it was just a little tiny one ... so I just threw my bow up in the tree and got up there. I had camouflage clothing on from head to toe, all the way, hat and everything ... and after I got in the tree I just froze, just sat as quiet as I could -- thought maybe they couldn't see me, because it was dark in the tree."

The light then made a large, sweeping half-circle maneuver to the east, around Shrum, moving over a canyon on the south side of the ridge. "Then I could see it," Mr. Shrum said, "and then it really scared me." Now, besides the bright light, he saw three illuminated, rectangular panels arranged in a vertically stepped-down formation. He saw no outline around the panels. The light remained in a fixed position to the right at a distance estimated at about 50 feet. These panels appeared as "flat surfaces" and sere an even distance apart. The quality of their lumines-cence was "like you would take aluminum foil and shake it -- you know, wiggle it against the fire ... and you would see the glis-tening, shimmering effect." He could see no "attachments" to either the three shimmering panels or the bright light. They remained motionless for about four or five minutes when "some-thing came out of the second one and all I could see was a kind of flash. Something went straight down the hill." Whatever it was that dropped from the second panel disappeared into the darkness of the underbrush. "It went pretty fast I saw a big flash of light as it left. I couldn't tell what it was. I just saw a dark ob-ject shoot right down and there was a flash when it came out." This second object then apparently moved around the witness in the dark, to the north side of the ridge. Shrum said, "I saw this little blinking light and I could see just a ... part of a dome on top and just a little light flashing on it." Asked specifically if he could see the object on the ground, Shrum said, "All I could see was the top -- it was a light, a flashing light on top."

A short time later, from the direction in which the dark ob-ject with a flashing light had landed, Shrum heard "all this crashing through the brush down the mountainside .... I was right on the point of the canyon and from here (the source of the noise) to the tree, it goes straight down into the canyon ... After about five minutes of the crashing through the undergrowth, I saw this first -- what do you call it -- person, or some kind of a guy all in some kind of light-colored, silver or whitish-looking uniform, with kind of puffs around the sleeves and joints." The being appeared to have on a helmet or some kind of a hood. "All I could see was a dark face." And it came to within a hundred feet of the tree, stopped, and appeared to be "messing around with the Manzanita ... I don't know what it was doing ... And then it was joined by another one just like it and they came down right below the tree, at the base of the tree, and were looking up at me."

Shrum described the eyes a similar to a welder's goggles -- dark and large, "big as silver dollars." The beings were about twelve feet from him, "straight down the tree." He said they had a kind of "signal set-up" with the object in the sky, which appeared to consist of a "cooing noise, something like an owl would make ... and I heard it from them on the hill and from the main ship, I guess. And, every time this noise would come from the ship ... they would do something else ... I just connected it. It might have been some owls some place, but I connected it."

While these two beings, described by the witness as "humanoid" in appearance, stood beneath the tree and stared up at him, Shrum heard more thrashing around in the brush, this time from a slightly different direction, along the ridge, "and I saw these big eyes coming, just like two flashlights hooked together." These glowing, luminous eyes were reddish-orange, "the color of fire." The light from the eyes lit up the face and jaw. No nose could be seen. This later arrival, while human in form, was short and stocky and appeared to be "robot-like," garbed in a kind of metallic uniform.

Shrum described the differences between this "ro-bot-like affair" and the two humanoids. "The one with the eyes (that) glowed ... was the same general shape, (but) a little bit taller." He said the robot was approximately five feet in height. "Where they were standing, down below me, it was hard to get a depth perception," he added.

The robot came right up under the tree "and stood there for awhile." The two humanoids remained down below the base of the rock, "just looking ... staring. They weren't doing anything else." This tableau was finally broken when the robot moved over to the remains of one of the fires and with its arm swept through the embers, scattering them.

Shrum described the hand, as it went through the fire, "like it was in joints, but it was like a hand -- you know, fingers and everything." He compared it to a "Medieval metal gauntlet." He said he was not able to see much detail from the neck down, just a generally human shape. He said that the way it moved and walked was not "flexible," as the movements of the humanoids were. The robot then moved back to the base of the tree and, while the humanoids watched, "it put one hand up to its mouth, I don't know why, and some kind of white vapor came out." He described the mouth as "square and hinged," somewhat like the mouth of a "Charley McCarthy dummy." The jaw seemed to hand open one to one-and-a-half inches most of the time. He could see that its head looked metallic.

"When this kind of white vapor, smoke, or whatever it was, came out, I blacked out ...." It was almost like a little breeze. He was upwind from me, so it just came up through the tree and acted like nitrogen (nitrous oxide) would, just (like) gas .... I never did smell anything. There was no smell of any kind, but I just kind of gasped for breath and then I blacked out and fell across my bow. That was the only thing that kept me in the tree, and when I woke up, I had the dry heaves ...." I figured they were out to get me then. I was going to be peaceful and quiet before that." Asked how long he thought he was out, Shrum said, "I don't think it was very long. I was half-conscious. I could feel myself fall over the bow, and then get right up. I doubt if it was more than a few minutes...."

"Then I lit a book of matches. I had six or seven books of matches with me; so, I lit a book of matches and threw it down, just to see if it would scare them away, and it did. They backed up; so, then I started going crazy with fire. I lit my hat and I guess I had a lot of hair oil on it because it really blazed up when I threw it down, right at the base of the tree, and they backed way up."

"They stayed a good 50 to 75 feet away. As soon as this blazed, I noticed that this ship (had) shot way up into the air. I didn't see it go up there. I just looked and it was up there. I could just barely see it then.... I guess it was kind of uncertain of itself and it backed up .... I could just make it out up there. And as soon as the fire started dying down ... they started coming back."

Shrum continued to light things and throw them down. "There is very little brush or anything around, and I was trying to catch it on fire .... I took everything out of my pockets and I ripped my camouflage clothing off, and I was burning it ... I just ended up with Levis and T-shirt on and shoes. I burned everything that would burn, and I ended up getting just one little fire

155

started ... But they stayed back as long as there was fire, a good blaze going. As soon as it died down, they'd come back in."

By this time, at least three hours had passed since darkness. "After burning everything I could burn," Shrum continued, "I tried shooting the robot with my bow, as he was the only one that was doing anything against me. The other two just stood and looked. The bow I've got has the velocity of a rife at that close range, twelve foot or so. So, I just pulled it back as far as I could, and hit him the first time, and it shoved him back against the rocks...."

"When it hit him, it was just like a big arc flash; it just flashed up real bright. I only had three arrows with me -- so that was all I shot. I shot him three times and all three times it pushed him back a little bit, with just a big, bright flash." When asked where it was aimed, Shrum said, "it was in the general vicinity of the heart .... He was right up against the rocks, so it didn't push him very far. And every time I shot, too, those others scattered a little bit. I guess it scared them a little." They did not attempt to fire anything in return, and Shrum at no time saw them carry firearms or anything that might be considered weapons.

After having used up his arrows, Shrum climbed to the top of the tree and tied himself to the trunk with his belt "just in case." From then on, the sequence of events became almost repetitious and continued throughout the remainder of the night. At some unspecified time, the first robot was joined by a second similar entity.

After he had secured himself to the tree, the robot approached the base of the tree and again emitted the gaseous vapor, which again blacked Shrum out. As he came to, Shrum discovered that the two humanoids were trying to climb up the base of the tree, which is twelve feet from the ground to the first limb. (Shrum stood on top of the four-foot-high rock at the base of the tree to gain access to the first limb.) "The two in white tried to boost each other up the tree," he explained. "Every time they would get up, I just grabbed a hold of the tree and (would) shake it as far as I could, bend the tree as far as I could .... As

156

soon as there would be the least little movement, they'd get down. They were, I guess, uncertain of just what happened, and it kept them down. I broke limbs off and threw them down, and I threw all the change I had in my pocket down, and anything I had with me I threw down, just to try and distract them. And this went on all night. As soon as the humanoids would leave, the robot would come up to the base of the tree and emit another cloud of vapor. "I'd be shaking the tree and then this gas would get me, and I'd black out, and then as soon as I'd wake up, I'd heave, and as soon as I'd come to my senses, they'd be just starting to get up the tree, so I knew I wasn't out very long, because I don't think they'd stay away that long." At one point, when Shrum threw down his canteen, one of the humanoids ran over and picked it up, examined it, and then tossed it aside.

"And I tried all kinds of goofy things," Shrum continued, "You know, just tried to distract them. I tried yelling and making all kinds of noises. I heard a bunch of coyotes off in the distance howling so I even tried to do that just to make them think there was more of me, you know, coming. I tried everything I could think of to try and distract them, but they just went around their business like I wasn't there …. They didn't seem to hear."

"When I would shout, these two in human form would look up, and all I could see was a black, flat-looking face with big, dark eyes. I couldn't tell the color, (but they) seemed extra large. And their face was just kind of black-looking. I couldn't see if they had a helmet on or not. They had white (on). I could see the top -- it looked like a suit they had on, over their head. All I could see was a black patch of face, and the eyes. I couldn't make out any features of the face." Asked if he could see a nose, Shrum first answered "no," but then changed his mind, adding, "Well, it seemed like it was awful low on their face, low and flat."

Besides the two robots (the first had been joined by a second), and the pair of humanoids near the tree, Shrum became aware of at least one other white-clad humanoid, possibly two, thrashing around in the brush. "I could see them going over a rock every once in a while, or hear them out in the brush, thrashing around .... It seemed like they were scouting for something, looking for something. I don't know what .... I'd say there were five or six (including the two robots) altogether. I might have seen the same one several times, I don't know."

Finally, just as the eastern sky was beginning to show the first pink traces of dawn, the two robots moved into a position at the base of the tree where "they stood, facing each other. You can see (from my photographs) this tree is pretty skimpy -- you can see down through it. Anyway, they stood facing each other and (it) just looked like a bunch of flashes going between them, like arc flashes ... they just lit up the whole area beneath that tree, going back and forth between these two."

Large volumes of fog began drifting upwards. Ac-cording to Shrum, it was so thick he could not see the robots "and I blacked out, colder than heck then. When I woke up, I was hanging just by my belt. My feet were hanging down and my head was hang-ing down. It was light, but the sun hadn't come up yet, and there was no sign of them."

Cold and exhausted, Shrum made his way out of the tree and picked up some of the items he had thrown down earlier, includ-ing his canteen and his bow and arrows. He found none of the coins he had tossed down. "I threw better than a dollar's worth of change down. I don't know if it was bright objects they picked up or not." There were remnants of burnt clothing and paper lying around, as well as the burnt patch of brush he had managed to set afire. He left the scene and finally found his way back to his friends at camp.

After having rested, he told his companions what had hap-pened. Alvarez, who had also briefly lost his way, said that sometimes after dark, he too had seen what he first thought was a shooting star, but he told Shrum, "I never saw a shooting star come in that low and last that long." He was convinced that his friend was telling the truth, as a result of his own sighting.

Later that same day, back at home, Shrum told his wife what had happened to him the previous night. His mother-in-law knew of a retired professor of astronomy at Sacramento State University, and Shrum made a report of the incident to this astronomer. The report was turned over to officials at Mather Air Force Base in a letter dated September 9.

On September 25, a Captain Cloud of McClelland Air Force Base, accompanied by an Air Force sergent, called on Shrum at this home and requested additional information. Shrum cooperated with the Air Force investigator and obligingly turned over one of the arrowheads, at the officer's request, for examination of metallic fragments that might have adhered to the tip. He also turned over his detailed annotated map of the area of the sighting, which gave the specific location of the incident reported.

Shrum told UFO investigator Paul Cerny that the Air Force officer suggested (1) that the witness might have encountered a group of Japanese in the area ("during the war we had trouble with the Japanese"); (2) that it might have been a group of teenagers "trying to pull a print;" and (3) that a group of Air Force trainees may have been out on bivouac in the mountains and could have been responsible for the incident. Suggestions of drinking and hallucinations were also touched upon by Captain Cloud. As for Japanese and teenaged pranksters, Shrum told Cerny that "I knew right there it wasn't Japanese ... and I told them I could just see a bunch of teenagers dressed in space suits way out in the middle of nowhere." He had called McClelland Air Force Base to find out if there had been military exercises that night in the Cisco Grove area, and was told there had not. Besides, he added, if that had been the case "they'd know some way of getting me out of there if they wanted me out."

Two or three weeks later, Shrum, with one of his hunting companions, his brother, and another friend, returned to the scene of the sighting. They found that the area had been "picked clean." He told Cerny that "this was all the stuff I left there. I know it was there on the morning when I left. I didn't take it back. This stuff was all gone. Nothing. It was cleaned out." However, they did find some cigarette and cigar butts lying around. It was Shrum's contention that, with the aid of his map, the Air Force had come in with a helicopter and "picked the place clean."

Captain Cloud has assured Shrum that his name would be kept confidential, as he sought no publicity over the incident. Yet some time after the official investigation, Shrum received letters from a UPI newsman who had heard of the report and wanted further details; his brother also received a letter of inquiry from a newsman, inquiring if he had been the one involved in the Cisco Grove UFO story. In November, Shrum received a letter requesting sighting details from investigator Jacques Vallee. None of these requests for information were acknowledged. Captain Cloud had promised the witness that his arrowhead would be returned following examination. It never was. According to a letter dated September 9, 1966, from Major James H. Aikman of the Blue Book Office of Information, no analysis was made of the arrowhead, and it had been "loaned to the Colorado UFO Study Group" and had not been returned to Shrum.

The two remaining arrowheads were loaned to NICAP for an examination and analysis of possible metallic fragments. Results of these tests proved negative.

APPENDIX C:
UFO "ROBOT" CASES

The files compiled over the years by civilian UFO organizations including NICAP, CUFOS, APRO, and MUFON contain numerous other UFO encounters involving robot-life entities, one of the first of which occurred in December 1957 when Mary M. Starr of Old Saybrook, Connecticut, reported seeing two robot-lke beings with "squarish heads" peering through the windows of a glowing, elliptical-shaped UFO that hovered near her home. After a few moments, the object zoomed away at a high rate of speed.

Five years later, in May of 1962, a woman living in La Pampa, Argentina, reported seeing a robot-like being coming out of a flying disk. When the creature saw her, it returned to the UFO and took off "at a tremendous speed." The woman's husband also saw the UFO. This was one of several similar reports in Argentina in 1962, which included a case in July involving a 17-year-old boy named Ricardo Limeres. While riding his motorcycle, the teen encountered a strange, 6-foot-tall being that moved like a robot, leaving deep tracks in the dirt. Limeres also noticed a bright white light low in sky in the direction the creature was moving.

The Shrum case occurred in September 1964, and the previously-mentioned Reeves case (See Chapter 6) in Brooksville, Florida happened on March 3, 1965. Four years later, in September 1969, a New Zealand woman named Terry Ennshyman reported seeing a landed flying saucer and an entity that looked like a robot. The creature guided her into the UFO and reportedly had sex with her.

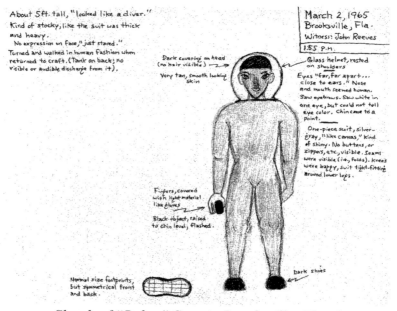

About 5ft. tall, "looked like a diver."
Kind of stocky, like the suit was thick and heavy.
No expression on face, "just stared."
Turned and walked in human fashion when returned to craft. (Tank on back; no visible or audible discharge from it).

Dark covering on head (no hair visible)
Very tan, smooth looking skin

March 2, 1965
Brooksville, Fla.
Witness: John Reeves
1:55 p.m.

Glass helmet, rested on shoulders
Eyes "far, far apart... close to ears." Nose and mouth seemed human. Saw eyebrows. Saw white in one eye, but could not tell eye color. Chin came to a point.

One-piece suit, silver-gray, "like canvas," kind of shiny. No buttons, or zippers, etc., visible. Seams were visible (i.e., folds). knees were baggy, suit tight-fitting around lower legs.

Fingers, covered with light material like gloves.

Black object, raised to chin level, flashed.

Normal size footprints, but symmetrical front and back.

Dark shoes

Sketch of "Robot" Seen in Brooksville, Florida

In November 1969 in Urubupunga, Brazil, a security guard reported encountering two tall robot-like creatures that communicated in shrill electronic tones. A large, metallic UFO was seen in the area a week later.

In April 1972 at Bents Basin, New South Wales, Australia, six young people encountered what looked like a 10-foot-tall robot. During the encounter, the car in which the youngsters were riding caught on fire shortly after they heard thumping noises on the roof. The robotic creature vanished suddenly without a trace.

In October 1973, three teenagers in Anthony Hill, Tennessee reported seeing an egg-shaped UFO and a "hairy" robot that walked with its hands up. An investigation of the scene later uncovered imprints from what appeared to be the landing gear of the UFO.

One of the most famous of all UFO abduction cases occurred at Pascagoula, Mississippi on October 11, 1973, and also involved robot-like beings. Calvin Parker and Charles Hickson were fishing on the Pascagoula River at 9 p.m. when they were approached by an egg-shaped object that hovered in the sky near them. Out of the ship floating toward them came three strange beings that were robot-like, with cone-shaped projections from front, back, and both sides of their heads.

The Pascagoula case was investigated by two individuals who also looked into the Shrum case -- Dr. James Harder of the Aerial Phenomena Research Organization (APRO) and Dr. J. Allen Hynek, representing the U.S. Air Force. About the case, Dr. Hynek said, "There was definitely something here that was not terrestrial."

Another robot sighting occurred on October 17, 1973 in Loxley, Georgia. A truck driver named Patterson claimed that both he and his truck were sucked up into a huge UFO. Once inside the ship, six tall "robots" dragged him out of his truck and seemed to be reading his mind. The next thing he knew, he was back in his truck and racing along the highway at 90 miles per hour. Two days later, on October 19, a small creature wearing a round helmet and whose head moved "like a robot" was seen in Ashburn, Georgia.

A year later, in June 1974, a major Canadian UFO case occurred in St. Cyrille de Wendover that also involved robot-like beings. A husband and wife were awakened at night by a large UFO hovering outside their rural home. Coming from the craft they saw fifteen "robots," each six feet tall with horizontal glowing red stripes across the chest. They moved mechanically and left the distinct impression that they were machines.

The area near Voronezh, Russia, experienced a wave of UFO sightings in September of 1989, several of which included reports of robot-like beings.

In truth, many UFO occupants described by witnesses over the years seem to have certain characteristics that appear robot-like. Some UFO researchers have suggested that most or all UFO occupants may be manufactured, cloned, or artificially created entities.

In his book *Architects of the Underworld*, Bruce Rux postulates the theory that most UFO occupants "exhibit the characteristics of artificial beings." He goes on to say, "Consider all the descriptions so far: glowing eyes; glowing bodies; identical appearances; no sex organs; no digestive tracts, no functioning mouths, and no anuses; metallic look; metallic feel; masklike faces with no expression; no discernible emotions; physically cold bodies; hobbling, awkward walks, stiff and mechanical, even overtly compared to 'automata' in some instances; hums, buzzes, and clicks for audible communication among themselves, like binary computers. What is the logical conclusion? ... [These creatures] are robots."

None other than possibly the world's most famous UFO researcher, Dr. J. Allen Hynek, added, "It is also peculiar that they [UFO occupants] would be able to adjust to our gravitational pull or breathe our air so easily. This could only mean that they are mechanical creatures -- robots -- or they originate from a habitat whose environment is very similar to ours here on Earth."

BIBLIOGRAPHY

Bloecher, Ted, and Paul Cerny. "The Cisco Grove Bow and Arrow Case of 1964." *International UFO Reporter*. 20:5, Winter 1995. pp. 16-22, 32. Print.

"California Man is Besieged By 'Occupants.'" *The APRO Bulletin*. July-August 1966, p. 5. Print.

Cerny, Paul C., and David Slette. "Cisco Grove, California, Bow and Arrow Case." Interview with Donald R. Shrum. Transcribed August 29, 1968. Print.

Cerny, Paul. Archive containing documents, correspondence, reports, articles, interviews, photographs, drawings, and illustrations pertaining to the Cisco Grove UFO Encounter (list of individual items follows).

Cerny, Paul. "Bow and Arrow Case: Cisco Grove, California, September 4-5, 1964." Report Prepared September 25, 1968. Print.

Clark, Jerome. "Brookeville Incident." *The UFO Encyclopedia*. Volume 3. Aston, PA: Omnigraphics, Inc., 1996. pp. 51-60. Print.

Hanlon, Donald B. "Questions on the Occupants." *Flying Saucer Review*. October-November 1966. Reprinted May 1968, pp. 64-66.

Keel, John A. "UFO Kidnappers." *Saga*. February 1967, pp. 53-54. Print.

Lorenzen, Coral. *The Flying Saucer Occupants*. New York:Signet, 1967. pp. 137-141.

Reichmuth, Steven. "The Cisco Grove Bow and Arrow Alien Encounter." *MUFON UFO Journal*. April 2007, pp. 3-6. Print.

Rux, Bruce. *Architects of the Underworld: Unriddling Atlantis, Anomalies of Mars, and the Mystery of the Sphinx*. Berkeley, CA: North Atlantic Books, 1996. pp. 165-167.

Shrum, Donald. Interview by Paul Cerny and David Slette (cassette tape recording). July 10-11, 1965.

Shrum, Donald and Judi. Interview by Ruben Uriarte (cassette tape recording). 2 September 2005.

Shrum, Donald and Judi. Interview by Ruben Uriarte (videotape recording). 2 September 2005.

Shrum, Donald and Judi. Personal collection of correspondence related to the Cisco Grove UFO Encounter. Loaned to Ruben Uriarte, 2011.

Shrum, Donald and Judi. Personal collection of photographs, drawings, articles, documents, and sketches related to the Cisco Grove UFO Encounter. Loaned to Ruben Uriarte, 2011.

National Investigations Committee on Aerial Phenomena (NICAP) and Center for UFO Studies (CUFOS). Archive containing documents, correspondence, reports, articles, interviews, photographs, drawings, and illustrations pertaining to the Cisco Grove UFO Encounter (list of individual items follows).

ARCHIVAL MATERIALS -- CUFOS/NICAP FILE

1964/9/9-Letter from Victor W. Killick, Astronomical Observatory, Sacramento City College. Xerox.

1964/9/25-Initial USAF message, Cit 5200P-I 9-271, 25 Sep 64, from 552 AEWCONWG McClellan AFB, Calif.

1964/9/25-USAF interview transcription between Shrum and SM Sgt. Barnes. 1 p. Xerox.

1964/10-Photos taken by witness of locale and tree. b/w prints.

1964/10-Project Blue Book 10073 record slip. Copy.

1964/10/2-Letter from USAF Col. T. de Jonckheere to McClellan AFB asking questions regarding case. Official file copy. FTD (TDEW) request.

1964/10/8-Letter from USAF Capt. Douglas W. Hawkins answering the Colonel's questions. Copy.

1964/11/13-Letter from Jacques Vallee to Shrum. Xerox.

1965/7/27-Letter from Cerny to Richard Hall re Shrum interview. Xerox.

1965/9I29-Letter from Cerny to Richard Hall re receipt of arrowheads. Xerox.

1965/10/17-Letter from James Harder to Shrum re request for interview. Xerox.

1965/10/25-Letter from Richard Hall to Cerny about NICAP cases, including Cisco Grove. Xerox. 1965/11/8-Note from Cerny re transmittal of arrowhead. Xerox.

1965/11/15-Letter from Richard Hall to Henry Kawecki re transmittal of arrowhead. Xerox.

1966/4/10-Letter from James Harder to Shrum re hypnotic regression proposal. Xerox.

1966/4/18-Letter from James Harder to Shrum re forthcoming interview at Harder's house on 4/25. Xerox.

1966/6/3-Letter from Richard Hall to Henry Kawecki re arrowhead analysis. Xerox.

1966/6/13-Letter from Henry Kawecki to Richard Hall re analysis of arrowhead. Xerox.

1966/6/17-Letter from James McDonald to Cerny re details of case. Xerox. Annotated by Cerny.

1966/6/23-Note from Cerny to Richard Hall transmitting McDonald letter.

1966/7/14-Letter from Cerny to James McDonald re details of case. Xerox. 2pp.

1966/7-8-A.P.R.O. Bulletin report, "California Man Is Besieged by 'Occupants,'" 1 p. Xerox. With Shrum's underlines to indicate which statements are erroneous.

1966/10/20-Letter from Richard Hall to Henry Kawecki re request to return arrowhead(s). Xerox.

1966/10/20-Letter from Richard Hall to Cerny re arrowhead analysis. Xerox.

1966/10/25-Letter from Cerny to Richard Hall re arrowhead analysis. Xerox. 1st page only.

1966/10/28-Letter from Henry Kawecki to Cerny re return of arrowheads. Xerox.

1966/11/23-Letter from Shrum to Cerny re investigation.

ARCHIVAL MATERIALS -- PAUL CERNY FILE

1964/7-Photo of Shrum at carnival (?).

1964/9/9-Letter from Victor W. Killick, Astronomical Observatory, Sacramento City College. Xerox.

1964/9/2S-Initial USAF message, Cit 5200P-I 9-271, 25 Sep 64, from 552 AEWCONWG McClellan AFB, Calif.

1964/9/25-USAF interview transcription between Shrum and SM Sgt. Barnes. 1 p. Xerox.

1964/10--Photos taken by witness of locale and tree. b/w prints and Xerox.

1964/10--Project Blue Book 10073 record slip. Copy.

1964/10/2-Letter from USAF Col. T. de Jonckheere to McClellan AFB asking questions regarding case. Official file copy. FTD (TDEW) request.

1964/10/8-Letter from USAF Capt. Douglas W. Hawkins answering the Colonel's questions. Copy.

1964/11/13-Lelter from Jacques Vallee to Shrum. Xerox. 1965/5/26-Lelter from Judi Shrum to Keyhoe re case. 5pp. Original.

196S/8/S-Letter from Judi Shrum to Cerny re case details. 1 p. Original.

1965/9/29-Letter from Cerny to Richard Hall re receipt or arrowheads. Copy.

1965/10/17-Letter from James Harder to Shrum re request for interview. Xerox.

1965/11/1S-Letter from Richard Hall to Henry Kawecki re transmittal of arrowhead. Xerox.

1966/4/10-Letter from James Harder to Shrum re hypnotic regression proposal. Xerox.

1966/6/13-Letter from Henry Kawecki to Richard Hall rc analysis of arrowhead. Xerox.

ALIENS IN THE FOREST

1966/7-8-A.P.R.O. Bulletin report, "California Man Is Besieged by 'Occupants,'" 1 p. Xerox. With Shrum's underlines to indicate which statements are erroneous.

1966/10/20-Letter from Richard Hall to Cerny re arrowhead analysis. Original.

1966/10/25-Letter from Cerny to Richard Hall re arrowhead analysis. Xerox. 3pp. Only first page relevant to case.

1966/10/28-Letter from Henry Kawecki to Cerny re return of arrowheads. Xerox.

1966/11/19-Letter from Cerny to Shrum re arrowheads. Copy. 1966/11/23-Letter from Shrum to Cerny re investigation. Xerox.

1967-Jim & Coral Lorenzen, *Flying Saucer Occupants,* pp. 137-41.

1967/2-*Saga* article by John Keel, "UFO Kidnappers," pp.53-54, with corrections by Shrum. Xerox and original.

1968-Northern California map with Cisco Grove circled.

1968-Lake Tahoe area map with camp and UFO area circled.

1968-Map [drawn by witness?] showing sighting area. Original.

1968-"Drawing of the UFO" by Shrum. Incorporated into Cerny report.

1968-Note re service no. of Capt. Carl F. Cloud. Undated.

1968/7/28-Letter from Bloecher to Cerny re questions about case in preparation for new volume of *UFO Evidence.* Xerox and annotated copy. 2pp.

1968/S/S-Additional notes from Cerny to Bloecher. Original.

1968/8/17-Letter from Bloecher to Cerny requesting transcript of taped interview. Xerox and copy.

1968/8/27-Letter from Cerny to Bloecher re case materials. Xerox.

1968/8/27-Letter from Bloecher to Cerny re case and USAF investigation. Annotated copy.

1968/8/28-Letter from Bloecher to Maj. James Aikman requesting details on USAF analysis. Xerox.

1968/8/29-Transcription of Cerny/Slette interview with Shrum. 19pp. + cover. Corrected.

1968/8-9-Transcription of Cerny/Slette interview with Shrum. 20pp. + cover.

1968/9/3-Letter from Cerny to Bloecher re transmitting first rough draft of case report. Xerox.

1968/9/5-Postcard from Cerny to Bloecher re first notification from Shrum.

1968/9/6?-Letter from Maj. James Aikman to Bloecher re USAF investigation. Xerox. Rec'd 9/19.

1968/9/7-Letter from Don & Judi Shrum to Cerny re case details. Xerox. 3pp.

1968/9/9-Letter from Bloecher to Cerny re rough draft. Copy. 2pp.

1968/9/12-Letter from Bloecher, to Maj. James Aikman re further questions. Xerox.

1968/9/12-Letter from Bloecher to Cerny re draft of report. Xerox and original (annotated by Cerny as a response).

1968/9/17?-Notes from Cerny to Bloecher re case. Mentions radiation checks and nightmares. Original. 1 p., 2-sided.

1968/9/17-Letter from Cerny to Bloecher re delay on Shrum report. Xerox and original.

1968/9/19-Letter from Cerny to Bloecher re more material to be sent. Xerox and original.

1968/9/20-Note from Judi Shrum to Cerny re transmittal of Alvarez statement.

1968/9/20-Letter from Alvarez to Cerny re Shrum. Transcription and original.

1968/9/20-Notes from Cerny to Bloecher re case details. Xerox and original. Original.

1966/12/19-Letter from Cerny to Shrum re hypnosis request. Copy.

ALIENS IN THE FOREST

1967-Jim & Coral Lorenzen, *Flying Saucer Occupants,* pp.137-41.

1967/2-Saga article by John Keel, "UFO Kidnappers," pp.53-54, with corrections by Shrum. Xerox and original.

1968-Northern California map with Cisco Grove circled. 1968--Lake Tahoe area map with camp and UFO area circled.

1968--Map [drawn by witness?] showing sighting area. Xerox.

1968?-Drawing of object by witness. Slightly different from other drawing. Xerox.

1968--"Drawing of the UFO" by Shrum. Incorporated into Cerny report.

1968/8/17-Letter from Bloecher to Cerny requesting transcript of taped interview. Original. Annotated.

1968/8/27-Letter from Bloecher to Cerny re case and USAF investigation. Annotated original.

1968/8-9-Transcription of Cerny/Slette interview with Shrum. 20pp. + cover.

1968/9/6?-Letter from Maj. James Aikman to Bloecher re USAF investigation. Xerox. Rec'd 9/9.

1968/9/7-Letter from Don & Judi Shrum to Cerny re case details. Original. 3pp.

1968/9/9-Letter from Bloecher to Cerny re rough draft. 1 p. Original.

1968/9/12-Letter from Bloecher to Maj. James Aikman re further questions. Copy.

1968/9/16-Letter from Don and Judi Shrum to Cerny re sending sketches made by Don. 2 pp. Original.

1968/9/9 Note from Bloecher to Cerny re Capt. Cloud and report's toc. Original. Undated.

1968/9/20--Letter from Alvarez to Cerny re Shrum. Transcription.

1968/9/23-Note from Ron Androukites, Naval Observatory, to NICAP re lunar data.

1968/9/23-Drawings of humanoid and robot, annotated by witness. Xerox. Received this date by Bloecher.

1968/9/23-Letter from Cerny to Bloecher re final report. Xerox and original.

1968/9/--Undated draft of Bloecher/Cerny report, with revisions in pen.

1968/9/--Undated Bloecher introduction and Cerny report, corrected by Cerny. Rough map (labeled #1) with corrections. Original.

1968/9/--Undated "Copies of drawings of the UFO by Witness." First drawing and revised drawing. Also, final drawing.

1968/9/-Copies of photos of tree, site, and arrowhead made at this time.

1968/9/24-Letter from Cerny to Bloecher re photos. Xerox.

1968/9/25-Artist's rendering of humanoid and robot, based on Shrum's drawings. Undated Xerox in Cerny report. Also, originals.

1968/9/25-"Bow and Arrow Case," report by Bloecher/Cerny. 9pp. + title page + toc.

1968/9/27?-Letter from Maj. James Aikman to Bloecher re USAF investigation. Original. Rec'd 10/11.

1968/11/--Letter from Bloecher to California Dept. of Fish and Game re hunting season. Copy.

1968/11/18-Letter from Bloecher to Roger N. Shepard at Stanford re hypnotic investigation. Xerox.

1968/11/18-Letter from Bloecher to Cerny re "occupant panel." Xerox.

1968/11/21-Letter from E. C. Fullerton, California Dept. of Fish and Game, to Bloecher. Original.

1968/11/24-Letter from Allen S. Mariner to Bloecher. Xerox.

1968/11/25-Letter from Allen S. Mariner to Anita Brothers re occupant panel. Xerox.

1968/11/27-Letter from Cerny to Bloecher re hypnosis and Shrum. Original.

1968/12/2-Letter from Bloecher to Cerny re Brothers' hypnosis of Shrum. Xerox.

1968/12/3-Letter from Roger N. Shepard to Bloecher re Brothers' hypnosis of Shrum. Xerox.

1968/12/6-Letter from Bloecher to Anita Brothers re occupant panel. Xerox.

1968/12/6-Letter from Bloecher to Cerny re Brothers meeting. Xerox.

1968/12/6-Letter from Bloecher to Roger N. Shepard re Brothers meeting. Xerox.

1969/3/20-Copy of slide of artist's conception of incident made.

1969/3/20-Official NICAP report form filled out by Shrum and received this date by Bloecher. Original.

1968/9/23-Drawings of humanoid and robot, annotated by witness. Original. 2pp. Received this date by Bloecher.

1968?-Undated drawing of UFO encounter area, showing Shrum in tree and aliens below. Undated original. Also another UFO drawing and Cerny notes.

1968/9/25-Artist's rendering of humanoid and robot, based on Shrum's drawings. Undated Xerox in Cerny report.

1968/9/25-"Bow and Arrow Case," report by Bloccher/Cerny. 9pp. + title page + toc.

1968/9/27?-Letter from Maj. James Aikman to Bloecher re USAF investigation. Xerox. Rec'd 10/11.

1968/10/14-Letter from Bloecher to Cerny re transmittal of Aikman letter. Original and copy.

1968/11/14-Letter from Lou [?] to Cerny re dubious existence of Capt. Cloud. Original.

1968/11/18-Letter from Bloecher to Cern7 re "occupant panel" Original.

1968/11/25-Letter from Allen S. Mariner to Anita Brothers re occupant panel. Copy.

1968/12/2-Letter from Bloecher to Cerny re Brothers' hypnosis of Shrum. Original.

1968/12/3-Letter from Roger N. Shepard to Bloecher re Brothers' hypnosis of Shrum. Xerox.

1968/12/6-Letter from Bloecher to Anita Brothers re occupant panel. Copy.

1968/12/6-Letter from Bloecher to Cerny re Brothers meeting. Original.

1968/12/6-Letter from Bloecher to Roger N. Shepard re Brothers meeting. Copy.

1968/12/21-Letter from Judi Shrum to Cerny re confidentiality. 1 p. Original.

1973/7/14-Note on Shrum by Cerny re nightmares. Original.

1973/10/10-Letter from Judi Shrum re physical effects. 6pp. Original.

1973/10/10-Letter from Judi Shrum re emotional effects. 11 pp. Original.

1973/11/--Letter from Don and Judi Shrum to Cerny re buzzing in his ears and NL seen on camping trip. 5pp. Original.

1974/3/30-Drawing of UFO by Shrum under hypnosis, Original.

1974/6/--Notes by Cerny on hypnotic session, including drawing of humanoid's hand. 4 pp. Original.

1975/10-Photo of Don and Judi Shrum.

1978/6/9-Notations on Shrum case, written by Cerny for Ronald Story's encyclopedia.

INDEX

177

Get the Real Story of Cowboys & Aliens!
Now Available at RoswellBooks.com

The Real Cowboys & Aliens
UFO Encounters of the Old West

By Noe Torres & John LeMay
Illustrated by Neil Riebe and Jared Olive

Praise for our book from the *Albuquerque Journal* daily newspaper: "Hey, Hollywood. If you're going to make a big-budget movie about extraterrestrial contact with Wild West cowpunchers, can't you at least try to get it right? John LeMay, a historian and author who lives in Roswell, says that of course spacemen explored our planet in the days of saddle-sore lawmen and swinging saloon doors. But it wasn't the cartoonish picture of evil planetary invaders, complete with hideous teeth and slimy hands emanating from their reptilian bellies that are portrayed in this Hollywood blockbuster. His book, The Real Cowboys & Aliens: UFO Encounters of the Old West sets the record straight, using information gathered from yellowed newspaper clippings from the 1800s to tell of numerous close encounters between farmers and cowboys on the range and mysterious visitors in flight." (*Albuquerque Journal*, Aug. 18, 2011, Page A1)

Long before graphic novels and Hollywood blockbusters, Cowboys and Aliens really did encounter each other, according to newspaper accounts and other historical documents of the 1800s. These unusual stories about UFO sightings in the Old West are revealed in a new book by Texas UFO researcher Noe Torres and New Mexico historian John LeMay. This critically-acclaimed book examines fourteen bizarre incidents, including the reported recovery in 1897 of a spaceship and its alien pilot in the Texas frontier town of Aurora.

Now available for print and for the Kindle at RoswellBooks.com and through online retailers including Amazon.com. Scan the QR code above to order your copy from Amazon today!

Ultimate Guide to the Roswell UFO Crash Now Available at RoswellBooks.com

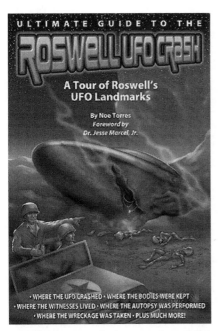

Best-selling author Peter Robbins says about our book, *"The Ultimate Guide* is deeply informative, well illustrated and consistently interesting. This is American history most Americans are completely unaware of and a public service to anyone who wants to walk the walk and experience the Roswell story via the actual locations where it occurred. Bravo Noe Torres and E.J. Wilson!"

Veteran Roswell researcher Kevin Randle says: "If you are planning to visit Roswell, this book tells you all you need to know about the UFO crash, the city and its character. It condenses the confusion of the case into an easily read book that will help anyone make the most of a visit to city and help understand what actually happened. A very nice addition to the Roswell literature."

For the first time ever, each of Roswell's UFO landmarks is carefully explored through witness interviews, photographs, and maps. The amazing story of the Roswell UFO crash is finally revealed by a close examination of where everything happened. Follow the trail of the world's most fascinating UFO case by walking in the very places where the eerie events of 1947 unfolded.

Now available for print and for the Kindle at RoswellBooks.com and through online retailers including Amazon.com. Scan the QR code here to order your copy from Amazon today!

UFO Crash on the Texas-Mexico Border
Now Available at RoswellBooks.com

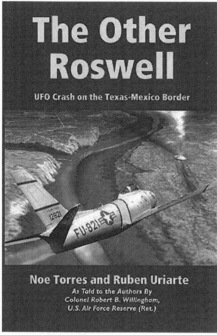

The Other Roswell

UFO Crash on the Texas-Mexico Border

Noe Torres and Ruben Uriarte
*As Told to the Authors By
Colonel Robert B. Willingham,
U.S. Air Force Reserve (Ret.)*

On a clear spring day in 1955, Air Force reservist Robert Willingham was piloting an F-86 fighter jet across West Texas when he saw an intensely bright UFO streak past his aircraft at over 2,000 miles per hour and then crash-land along the banks of the Rio Grande River, where he later found smoldering, twisted wreckage that convinced him the object was not of the Earth.

Dr. Bruce Maccabee, world-class UFO researcher, says about this book, "One of the world's most interesting UFO crash retrieval stories. I believe that the reader will find this book important support for the idea that Alien Flying Craft have crashed on earth and have been retrieved and covered up by the United States government."

The Other Roswell: UFO Crash on the Texas-Mexico Border discloses for the first time ever, the eyewitness testimony of Colonel Willingham, who says that he chased a UFO across Texas, saw it crash to the earth near Del Rio, Texas, and later visited the crash site.

You've heard about this amazing book on *Coast to Coast AM* with George Noory, the Jeff Rense program, and other shows we have done. Now, you  can read the complete story from the eyewitness himself. Available for print and for the Kindle at RoswellBooks.com and through online retailers including Amazon.com. Scan the QR code here to order your copy from Amazon today!

Mexico's Roswell – Revised 2nd Edition
Now Available at RoswellBooks.com

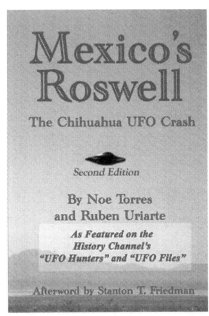

On August 25, 1974, along the Rio Grande River near the Texas border town of Presidio, a thunderous explosion in the sky shattered the stillness of the warm summer night. An unidentified flying disc traveling at 2,000 miles per hour collided with a small airplane heading south from El Paso, Texas. The flaming wreckage of both aircraft fell to the Mexican desert below and immediately became the object of an intense recovery effort by military forces from both Mexico and the United States. This book reveals the shocking story of that night's historic events, as two governments raced to a remote corner of the Chihuahuan Desert in an effort to recovery evidence of a technology from beyond the Earth. The 2nd edition has been fully revised and updated to include the latest information on this incredible case.

PRAISE FOR MEXICO'S ROSWELL: "Amazing! This story is wilder than the U.S. Roswell. This book is an amazing piece of work." -- George Noory, *Coast to Coast AM*, 8/20/2007.

"Well-researched, well written, and well constructed as a whole ... A definite must-read." -- *MUFON UFO Journal*, Sept. 2008, p. 15.

"Noe Torres and Ruben Uriarte are to be commended for taking on this task... I hope that this book will encourage others to come forward." -- Stanton T. Friedman, Nuclear Physicist and Original Roswell UFO Researcher

This incredible story was featured on the History Channel's *UFO Files*, *UFO Hunters*, and *UFOs of the 70s*.

Available for print and for the Kindle at RoswellBooks.com and through online retailers including Amazon.com. Scan the QR code here to order your copy from Amazon today!

Fallen Angel – Laredo UFO Incident
Now Available at RoswellBooks.com

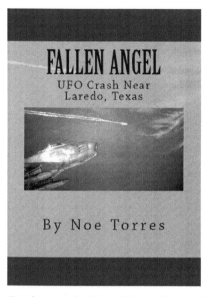

On July 7, 1948, U.S. military aircraft chased a fast-moving, 90-foot-diameter silver disc across Texas before watching it crash about 30 miles south-southwest of Laredo, Texas. Known as the "Laredo UFO Crash," this case occurred almost exactly one year after the famous Roswell UFO Incident and holds much of the same mystery and intrigue.

Witnesses later claimed that the military recovered a "fallen angel," a crashed alien ship and at least one non-human occupant.

For the first time ever, this book presents all of the evidence regarding this hotly-debated UFO case. First unveiled at the Laredo UFO Conference held on November 5, 2011 at Texas A & M International University, this book contains one of the least-known but most impressive UFO stories ever.

Author Noe Torres has appeared on the History Channel's "UFO Hunters," George Noory's "Coast to Coast AM," the Jeff Rense Program, and many other shows. His previous books include the widely-acclaimed "The Real Cowboys & Aliens: UFO Encounters of the Old West", "Ultimate Guide to the Roswell UFO Crash", and "Mexico's Roswell." He is currently director of the Mutual UFO Network (MUFON) in South Texas.

Available at RoswellBooks.com and through online retailers including Amazon.com. Scan the QR code above to order your copy from Amazon today!

Where the Weird Things Are!
Now Available at RoswellBooks.com

The year was 1997 and some 40,000 tourists and reporters descended upon the desert town of Roswell, New Mexico, where 50 years earlier a flying saucer is said to have crashed. Even today, UFOs and "Little Green Men" remain Roswell's top tourist draw. This book takes a fresh new look at the Roswell Incident from an "insider's perspective" - that of lifelong Roswell resident John LeMay, a historian and author born and raised in the Alien Capital of the World. His childhood being filled with tales of flying saucers and alien autopsies, John grew up knowing several key Roswell eyewitnesses, including Robert Shirkey, who said he saw UFO debris being loaded onto a B-29 bomber at the Roswell Army Air Field in 1947.

In the first part of this remarkable new book, John's keen insight and marvelous sense of humor deliver a fresh new angle on the story of the Roswell UFO crash and on some of Roswell's other, lesser-known mysteries.

Read about the "alien ghost" that haunts the New Mexico Rehabilitation Center; the "Second" Roswell UFO Crash of 1949; Bottomless Lakes where cars sink into the depths and monsters emerge to the surface; the Headless Horsewoman of Lover's Lane, a Victorian Era Spook with an axe to grind against young lovers; and much more!

Available in print and for the Kindle at RoswellBooks.com and through online retailers including Amazon.com. Scan the QR code above to order your copy from Amazon today!

Made in the USA
Middletown, DE
06 October 2022

12078905R00108